A! FOR LIFE

100+ Ways to Use Artificial Intelligence
to Make Your Life Easier,
More Productive...
and More Fun!

CELIA QUILLIAN
Creator of @SmartWorkAI

ADAMS MEDIA
NEW YORK   AMSTERDAM/ANTWERP   LONDON   TORONTO   SYDNEY   NEW DELHI

Dedication

For Neil

Adams Media

An Imprint of Simon & Schuster, LLC

100 Technology Center Drive

Stoughton, Massachusetts 02072

First Adams Media trade paperback edition
January 2025

ADAMS MEDIA and colophon
are registered trademarks of
Simon & Schuster, LLC.

For information about special discounts
for bulk purchases, please contact Simon &
Schuster Special Sales at 1-866-506-1949 or
business@simonandschuster.com.

The Simon & Schuster Speakers Bureau can
bring authors to your live event. For more
information or to book an event, contact
the Simon & Schuster Speakers Bureau at
1-866-248-3049 or visit our website at
www.simonspeakers.com.

Interior design by Kellie Emery

Manufactured in the United States of
America

1 2024

Library of Congress Cataloging-in-
Publication Data has been applied for.

ISBN 978-1-5072-2339-0
ISBN 978-1-5072-2340-6 (ebook)

Contents

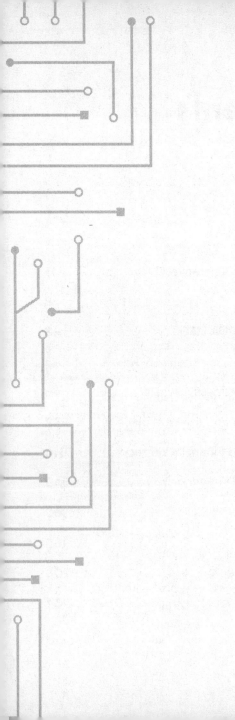

Acknowledgments

Thanks first to my editor at Adams Media, Colleen Mulhern, who saw the opportunity for a book with a mission to teach *everyone* about AI's possibilities and took a chance on this first-time author to make that idea a reality. To my development editor, Laura Daly, thank you for your expert guidance in structuring this book for the best possible reading experience. Julia DeGraf, thank you for your eagle eyes in the copyediting process.

To my fourth-grade teacher, Diane Dalbo, who fostered my love of writing and the idea that I *could* write a book one day, and to all the teachers and mentors who came after supporting and developing my creative storytelling passion: Thank you. To Professor Marina Cooley, thank you for introducing me to TikTok and "sticky storytelling"—these concepts are what helped build @SmartWorkAI. To Shawn Coyne, Kate Dramis, and Alan Clarke, thank you for your guidance and advice in the writing and publication process.

To my family, friends, and neighbors, thank you for your encouragement, your questions about AI, and your anecdotes. Through sharing all of these, you helped me (perhaps unknowingly) to write an even better book. Especially to my grandmother, Celia Patrick, and my great-aunt, Sarah Martin, thank you for your curiosity in understanding this new-fangled technology, and your patience in my explanations. You helped me make this book as accessible as possible to nontechnical readers.

To my parents, Henry and Deanie Quillian, thank you for everything—for raising me to be curious, for supporting my creative pursuits, and for instilling in me a desire to help others.

And finally to my amazing husband, Neil Bancherosmith, thank you for your constant support on this wild journey—for keeping me inspired, motivated, *fed*, in good humor, and in good health throughout the late nights, weekends, and very early mornings of this writing process. I love you.

Introduction

Ever since OpenAI's explosive launch of ChatGPT, it seems we cannot go a day without hearing some mention of AI and how it is changing the world around us. While the transformative promise of AI is exciting, it can also feel overwhelming. And all that jargon? No, thank you. How do these AI tools work anyway? And how would an everyday person even use AI?

That's where this book comes in. While much of the chatter around AI is in the realm of business, this collection will focus instead on the wide variety of ways generative AI can make your personal life easier, more productive, and even more fun. With it, you'll learn to outsource the tedious tasks of your day-to-day life to an expertly efficient and collaborative partner—AI! By learning to harness the power of AI, you can focus even more of your energy on your hobbies, social life, and…well, living!

You'll first learn some background information on the strengths and limitations of AI, an overview of popular free tools to start with (including ChatGPT), and easy-to-follow guidance on how to write effective prompts that will get AI working for you. Then we'll dive into the good stuff: the dozens of specific ways you can use AI, spanning a wide array of categories such as health and wellness, career development and the workplace, personal finance, relationships and social skills, and travel. For example, you'll learn how to use AI to:

- Plan a vacation itinerary
- Suggest recipes based on ingredients you have on hand
- Optimize your budget
- Customize resumes and cover letters
- Learn and practice a foreign language
- Tell your kids customized bedtime stories
- And so much more!

Each two-page entry features information on exactly how AI can help you complete each task, sample prompts to start with (which you can test by simply reading aloud to your favorite free AI app), and suggestions for how to make the prompts your own for even better results. On top of that, you'll find dozens of quick suggestions for each category, from finding ingredient substitutions to preparing a packing list. Most importantly, as you read, you'll naturally begin to imagine even more new and inventive ways to use AI!

AI is here to stay—so you might as well learn how to make it work for you. *AI for Life* equips you with the knowledge and confidence to create your own powerful, personalized prompts and make generative AI your hardworking assistant. Start harnessing AI to help you streamline tasks, take chores and tasks off your plate, spark your creativity, and give you the gift of more free time!

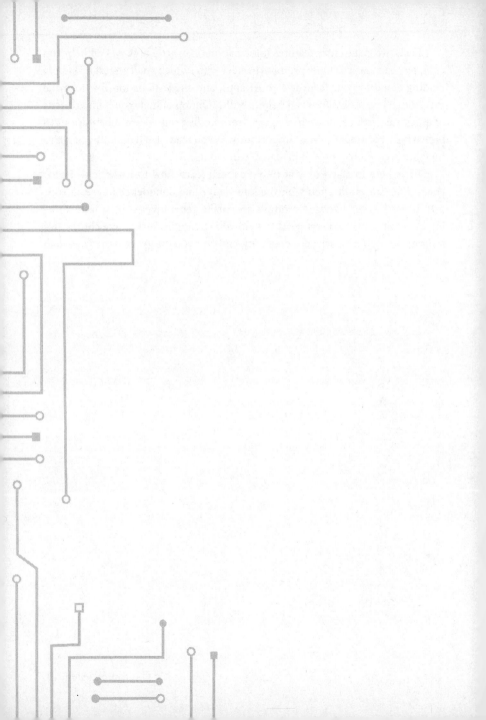

⊷ PART 1 ⊶

Understanding AI

Ready for a crash course on generative AI? Don't be intimidated—you won't be buried in jargon or drowning in technical theory. In Part 1, I've distilled the most critical details into a single approachable chapter. You'll learn what you, as the *user* of AI, most need to know to effectively engage with it, including understanding the strengths and weaknesses of generative AI.

You'll also get oriented with the basic AI terms, discover how these tools work, and meet some popular (and free!) generative AI programs that you can use in conjunction with the use cases in Part 2. We'll even cover the varied capabilities of these tools, from voice communication to AI image generation and more. Finally, you'll learn how to engage with AI through effective prompt-writing techniques, shortcuts, and tips.

This part will set you up with a strong foundation for all of your future AI interactions, both simple and more complex. Let's dive in!

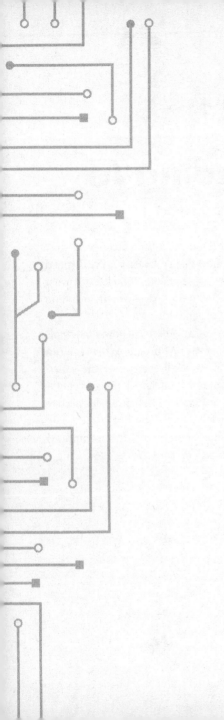

CHAPTER 1

Getting Started with Generative AI

AI is far more than a buzzword—it is a rapidly evolving technology that is still in its early phases of adoption. Before you know it, however, these tools will be as commonplace as the Internet is today.

Whether you are entirely new to generative AI tools like ChatGPT or you have played around with these tools but weren't quite sure how best to use them, understanding the fundamentals of how they work (and how to work with them) is essential to getting the most out of them. Before we dive into the various ways you can leverage AI to enhance your daily life, this chapter will unpack everything you need to know to "work smart" with generative AI, from how it works to how to interact with it to get what you want. My goal in this chapter is to teach you how AI works and how to work with AI effectively so that you can harness its power both now and in the future as AI technology continues to evolve.

Artificial Intelligence Is Not New

Whether you realize it or not, you have likely been benefiting from artificial intelligence programs for a while now. For years, search engines like Google and Yahoo! have been powered by sophisticated AI techniques, as have the speech-recognition functionalities within Apple's Siri or Amazon's Alexa. Whenever your smartphone suggests a word or spelling correction, you have AI to thank. Similarly, those custom-tailored recommendations in streaming platforms? AI. And this is just a sampling of the many ways we have all been leveraging AI in our lives.

Yet *AI* and *artificial intelligence* have only recently become huge buzzwords in daily conversations. And all this recent "AI this" and "AI that" chatter in the public space can be traced back to the record-shattering public launch of OpenAI's ChatGPT on November 30, 2022. According to a *UBS* report, the launch attracted one million users in its first week and over one hundred million within its first two months. Thanks in part to its accessibility; ease of use; and, of course, the "Wow" factor, suddenly everyone had at least heard of the term *AI*, and not in the context of science fiction. With all the buzz circulating about this previously little-known company, OpenAI, the big guys (Google, Microsoft, and Meta) and others started to enter the market with generative AI tools of their own.

What Is Generative AI?

To start, *artificial intelligence* is a blanket term used to describe when a machine is programmed to simulate human intelligence, learning, or problem-solving. *Generative AI* refers to a class of artificial intelligence tools that can "generate" new content based on requests (inputs or "prompts") they receive.

The Basics of Large Language Models

ChatGPT and other tools we'll discuss in Part 1 are generative AI applications powered by "large language models." An LLM is a type of AI model that is built to process, respond to, and interact with human language. These tools can therefore respond to your inputs in natural language. There are also many generative AI tools that leverage LLM technology to perform tasks like generating images, music, and even video, based on the human language requests given to them.

How do LLMs work? In simple terms, when you put a new text-based request into tools like ChatGPT, the LLM calls upon its "training" (which consists of a *massive* amount of data) to predict what word, and each subsequent word, would best answer the initial request. It's basically like a very, *very* advanced auto-complete. But instead of generating a single word or short phrase at a time, it can generate hundreds of words in a tidily structured format, customized to whatever your initial request was. Put yet another way, these tools are just really good at mimicking human language patterns.

A Human-Machine Partnership

If analogies are more your thing, imagine if you would, that a large language model is like a human writer. This writer is an expert on the writing styles of thousands of authors. They studied writing extensively and have developed an incredible skill of mimicking the particular styles of great writers. So if you hire this person to write a short story in the style of, say, Charles Dickens, they can provide something that sounds very much like something Dickens might have written! But let's say you aren't thrilled about a particular plot twist, so you give some feedback to your writer friend and ask them to change the storyline a bit. When they do, the second draft is even better, thanks to their expertise and your feedback.

Because of an LLM's ability to recognize and mimic human language patterns, working with generative AI tools is much like this interaction. You make a request, and the tool's model draws upon its "knowledge" and creates something based upon your request. If you subsequently ask for the tool to adjust its outcome, it will oblige and deliver something new according to that feedback.

Conversational Power

Why are LLMs able to respond to feedback in this way? This ability to adjust to feedback is largely thanks to the "context window" of the large language model. A context window is effectively the amount of "memory" an LLM has for your conversation in a given chat. Context windows are measured in "tokens." For simplicity's sake, think of a "token" as your average 5-letter word. An 8,000-token context window, the lowest context window limit you'll encounter among the free tools mentioned in this book, would therefore be the equivalent of about 27 pages of text in an average book. That's still a pretty lengthy conversation! Meanwhile, other LLMs offer even larger windows, like GPT-4o (128k), Claude 3.5 Sonnet (200k), or even more than one million tokens with Gemini's 1.5 Pro model, available with the paid version of Gemini.

The LLM acquires more and more "context" the longer you chat within it. Everything you input into the chat (including attachments) and everything your AI tool generates back in response contribute to the context memory, which it references with each subsequent response to you. Kind of like "temporary training data" layered on top of the existing model, which it can only maintain within the bounds of its context window.

If you chat too long and reach the limit of your context window (or if you attach large files in your chats), however, you might notice that your tool starts to become a little "confused" if you reference something said in the same chat too long ago, and it may need to be reminded of the context it has lost. This is not totally unlike a human interaction—after all, a detail mentioned to a coworker in a meeting yesterday is often more easily remembered than a detail from a month ago!

The Strengths of Generative AI

This book will focus primarily on the many ways you can use generative AI tools like ChatGPT, which primarily provide text-based responses to your inputs, though we will touch on AI-generated images as well. If you want to create or learn about something that can be accomplished or communicated with written text, ChatGPT (and other AI tools like it) can do it. Generative AI tools leveraging LLMs are particularly strong at all of the following:

- **Leveraging a vast knowledge base:** LLMs just "know" a lot of stuff. Imagine being able to understand all of the knowledge within all of the books in a massive library—that's basically what ChatGPT allows you to do. Similar to search engines, generative AI can unlock access to vast amounts of information in record time, helping you learn, create, and even think faster.

- **Comprehending your requests:** LLMs have a great depth of understanding for human requests. Based on the words we use in our "chats" with these tools, LLMs can predict what answers and structure of output will best fit our needs. They can even do this if your requests are long and rambling. (Although the best results do come from well-structured and clear prompts, which you will learn more about in this book!)

- **Having a "memory" and ability to understand context:** Generative AI tools can recall your conversation within a chat so that you can continually build upon your initial request. Basically, you can have a conversation within an AI application, and it will not "forget" what was said moments after you said it—just like you would with a human expert on a subject you are hoping to learn more about. There *is* a limit to the amount of "memory" these tools have for a given chat (as mentioned earlier), but for the most part, the conversational nature of these tools makes them very easy to work with.

- **Collaborating creatively:** Because of their vast knowledge base and skill at recognizing patterns in data, LLMs are adept at idea generation and problem-solving while also being excellent collaborators. Similarly, their database and training recognition allows them to easily adapt to new requests and styles, effortlessly "role-playing" as any type of persona you'd ask for an answer to a given query.

- **Conversing in many languages:** Because their training data also includes materials in a variety of languages, generative AI tools are also strong translators, especially for popular world languages. ChatGPT, for example, can understand, translate, and respond to requests in more than eighty languages.

- **Affordability and accessibility:** Accessibility is the final major strength of these tools. While there are "paid" subscriptions for most popular AI tools to access even more advanced features, most popular generative AI applications provide some level of free access to anyone with access to the Internet.

The Limitations of Generative AI

Like a Swiss Army knife, we've established that generative AI is good at a lot of things. But also, just like if you misuse a Swiss Army knife, if you use generative AI the wrong way or you don't fully understand the proper way to leverage it, things won't go well. While these tools are capable of performing a huge number of helpful tasks and have access to a huge wealth of knowledge, they are not perfect. Let's briefly review some common misconceptions about generative AI and unpack its weaker areas so that you know these ahead of time and can work around these limitations.

AI "Hallucination"

When working with these tools for the first time, it can be easy to fall for a common misconception: that because they have access to so much knowledge, because their answers are generated so quickly and confidently, and because so much of what they say is correct, these tools are *always* correct. This just isn't the case. While these models are adeptly trained and usually produce factual results, it's important to always remember that these tools are capable of what's called "hallucination," or generating incorrect or perhaps even nonsensical information. After all, these are predictive models, and what prediction is correct 100% of the time?

Generative AI's answers tend to be most factual when the topic covers subjects that have been well documented or topics that have a wealth of publicly available information. But the model is more likely to hallucinate when asked about highly specialized or niche topics (for example, brand-new scientific studies or specific court cases) or when asked about recent events that happened after the particular model's training data cut off.

Furthermore, if you ask ChatGPT to generate a bibliography of sources for what you have discussed in your chat, it will happily oblige with something that looks like a typical bibliography. But when you fact-check with a short Google search, you may be shocked to find that some of the research papers or articles referenced simply don't exist!

SOLUTION

Because of AI hallucinations, when engaging with generative AI tools—especially when using them as a jumping-off point for research or workplace scenarios—it's important to fact-check information in your outputs against a secondary source to be certain the information you received is accurate. It all comes down to the model's training and the quality of the data.

Even if the AI has web-browsing features, you should always click through to the source to determine both the source's credibility on the topic and the degree of accuracy in the AI summary of the source's contents.

Mathematics

The predictive nature of generative AI is also the reason why the popular tools in this book may be able to help with basic math questions (like $4 + 10 = 14$) but may struggle when asked to do more complex calculations ($4{,}229 \times$

2,099,032). These tools are not calculators. They are just predicting—based on the data and patterns their sophisticated algorithms have been trained on—what character or word is most likely to follow the previous one. Generally speaking, when approaching math problems, you may be able to leverage AI to teach you *the method* for doing the math, but not for calculating the thing itself.

SOLUTION

If you really need help with a math calculation, ChatGPT has a data analysis feature that can be accessed through ChatGPT Plus (and also through free ChatGPT, up to a certain limit). This feature within ChatGPT has been specifically trained to be able to perform more advanced calculations by running a Python script when answering mathematical queries.

Human Logic and Humor

When working with these generative AI tools, you'll likely quickly discover they just aren't very funny, even when you ask them to be. Their jokes can be a bit nonsensical, and their puns often don't make much sense, especially when bridging two topics that aren't regularly connected. The absurdity of their answers when asked to be funny is probably one of the (unintentionally) funniest things about them. While these tools seem to comprehend and understand the common structure of jokes or riddles, the punchlines just fall flat.

The same can be true for human logic—those things that we inherently know or can use logic to figure out. One example? When I asked ChatGPT's older GPT-3.5 model the question "If I started with 5 sticks, then I cut each stick in half, how many stick ends do I have now?" As humans, we can see in our mind's eye the 5 sticks being cut in half, each turning into two separate sticks with 2 separate ends. So *we* know the answer must be 20. But GPT-3.5 very confidently said that the answer was 10. I've found that GPT-4, a more advanced model, gets this answer right more often, but it still misses the mark regularly.

This lack of logic can be spotted in AI image and video generation as well, where images generated by AI may feature some nonsensical visual elements like an extra finger on a person in the photo, a piece of furniture that is unrealistically proportioned, or a moving image that does not quite accurately reflect the laws of gravity. Such details, while becoming harder and harder to spot as these tools get better, can be helpful tells for spotting AI images in the wild.

So why is generative AI not great at humor or logic? In short, both often involve nuance and an understanding of human experience that AI does not have (save for whatever is available in its training data). While it can mimic some logic, humor, and empathy, it is not truly capable of a human level of understanding that we get from lived experiences.

SOLUTION

Be mindful of ChatGPT's limitations when it comes to humor and logic. If you really need help with a joke or a pun, asking it to brainstorm 5 or 10 different attempts will make it more likely that at least one of these jokes "lands." Similarly, if its logic seems off, you can always provide it feedback to get it back on track. Still be wary however—these tools aim to please, and they can still be confidently illogical in certain scenarios, even after giving such feedback.

Data Privacy

It is important to understand that generative AI tools "read" and process the text inputs you give them to generate their responses. This entered data may then be stored in some way, as oftentimes these inputs are used to help improve the performance of the model and build future versions of the model that have even better responses and depth of natural language understanding. Beyond that, as with most companies that store data, there's always a risk of a potential data breach.

SOLUTION

As you use generative AI, you should avoid including any deeply personal or sensitive information in your text prompts (think: your full legal name, social security numbers, banking information, etc.). Also, never upload copyrighted material. In work scenarios, you should also understand your company's perspective on the use of these tools by talking with your data privacy team. As a rule of thumb, it would be unwise to upload any private customer data, company financial statements, or proprietary information into these models.

AI and the Ethics of Plagiarism

It's also important to think about the ethical considerations you should keep in mind when leveraging generative AI. Perhaps the most important thing is that even though AI *can* create complete stories, guides, blog posts, essays, and any other piece of writing for you, publishing that work as your writing without creating significant edits and disclosing the use of generative AI could be considered plagiarism and ethically wrong.

Presenting unedited AI-generated text as your own may not only violate academic integrity and impact your credibility as a professional, but it can (perhaps inadvertently) also lead to the spread of misinformation if you did not check the text for AI hallucination.

Furthermore, while generative AI tools are designed to produce original responses, there is a risk that what they generate could mimic existing materials a bit too closely, putting you at risk for plagiarism if you decide to publish these outputs as your own work.

SOLUTION

While at the time of this writing, there are not yet any strict laws or regulations about the proposed use of AI-generated content, there are expected to be laws passed on the subject in the not-too-distant future, as government bills and state-level legislation have started to be introduced. Therefore, when using AI to create content that you intend to publish, it is best to be transparent and disclose to what extent the content was AI-generated or what was AI-generated then vetted for accuracy or more deeply edited.

Inherited Bias

Another important consideration to keep in mind when using generative AI is that these tools will be as biased as the materials they were trained upon. For example, if its training data is not diverse or balanced across cultures, genders, and ethnicities, the content it generates might disproportionately favor or reflect the experiences of certain groups over others, or it might offer perspectives that align more with certain viewpoints. Inadvertently, this could lead to responses that perpetuate stereotypes or neglect certain perspectives.

While inherited bias certainly also exists in AI's textual responses, it is most easily illustrated with the image generation capabilities of these tools. When, for example, I asked ChatGPT Plus to create an image of "Four distinct and diverse pictures of a professional," even though I emphasized "diverse" in my prompt, it generated four pictures of a white man wearing uniforms for different kinds of professions. (In my experience thus far, if you want results showing women or people of different ethnic backgrounds, you must state that explicitly in your prompt.) As another example, ask to create an image of a "French person," and you'll most often get a deeply stereotypical image of a white man in a beret and black-and-white striped shirt, carrying a baguette and cheese, in front of the Eiffel Tower.

SOLUTION

Understanding the presence of bias in the training data of generative AI tools can empower you to use these tools more responsibly and ethically. It's your responsibility to actively look for and address any potential bias issues, whether in text, images, or any other output.

Popular AI Tools

In the past few years, countless generative AI products have entered the marketplace, providing free access to the public to use. Businesses have adapted as well, integrating generative AI into their internal processes or even their products. As of this book's writing, ChatGPT remains the most popular and most recognized AI tool among the general public. The free version of ChatGPT is great at a variety of tasks, but it has certain limitations that the free versions of other tools (or ChatGPT Plus, the paid version) can accomplish.

In this section, you'll learn some of the most popular free AI tools, how to sign up for them, and the variety of features available that can be leveraged for use cases in Part 2.

Generative AI Tools Mentioned in This Book

CHATGPT (FREE) AND CHATGPT PLUS (PAID)

- **What?:** A generative AI chatbot launched by OpenAI. "GPT" stands for "Generative Pre-Trained Transformer." Yes! It is a mouthful.

- **How?:** Sign up with an email address at https://chatgpt.com or download the official ChatGPT app by OpenAI from your smartphone's app store (available for iOS and Android). The official app is called "ChatGPT," and the description will say it is "The official app by OpenAI."

- **Models used:** GPT models: GPT-4o mini (Free), GPT-4 (Plus), GPT-4o (Free—Limited and Plus), and o1-Preview (Plus), their latest model boasting more advanced logic and reasoning skills in exchange for a slower response time.

MICROSOFT COPILOT (FREE) AND COPILOT PRO (PAID)

- **What?:** A generative AI chatbot developed by Microsoft and released originally as "Bing Chat."
- **How?:** Sign up with an email address on your desktop or your mobile browser at https://copilot.microsoft.com, or in mobile app form for iOS and Android in the app store.
- **Models used:** GPT models: GPT-4, and GPT-4o

GOOGLE GEMINI (FREE) AND GEMINI ADVANCED (PAID)

- **What?:** A generative AI chatbot developed by Google and released originally as "Google Bard."
- **How?:** Sign up with an email address at https://gemini.google.com. You can also access Google Gemini in the iOS or Android app store by downloading the "Google" mobile app.
- **Models used:** Gemini models

CLAUDE BY ANTHROPIC (FREE) AND CLAUDE PRO (PAID)

- **What?:** Claude is a family of LLMs and generative AI chatbot developed by AI startup company Anthropic.
- **How?:** Sign up with an email address at https://claude.ai. The "Claude by Anthropic" app is also available for download in the iOS or Android app stores.
- **Models used:** Claude models: Haiku, Sonnet (Free), Opus (Paid)

PERPLEXITY AI (FREE) AND PERPLEXITY PRO (PAID)

- **What?:** A conversational AI-powered search engine launched by a privately held software company of the same name. Gives users the ability to focus and refine AI-summarized search results to only reference certain types of sources like academic papers, Reddit threads, video, and more, depending on preference.

- **How?:** Sign up with an email address at https://perplexity.ai or via the iOS or Android app of the same name.

- **Models used:** Combination of GPT and Claude models (more recent and premium models on paid version)

META AI (FREE)

- **What?:** An AI chatbot within Meta's Facebook, Instagram, and WhatsApp applications, as well as via a dedicated website.

- **How?:** Visit https://meta.ai on your web browser and log in with your Instagram or Facebook account. Alternatively, access via your messaging tools and search bars within your Facebook, Instagram, or WhatsApp applications. Its icon looks a bit like a glowing blue and purple donut!

- **Models used:** Llama models developed by Meta

Keep in mind this is by no means an extensive list and that the offerings across free and paid tool versions (as well as their price points) tend to change as the companies behind these tools develop more capabilities and even more powerful models. Now and in the years to come, you'll likely encounter specialized "chatbots" on other websites, in phone applications (and in your smartphones themselves!), and more. The good news is, no matter which tool you use, the theory behind how you use and prompt them remains the same!

Features and Considerations

Following is a breakdown of extra capabilities found within some or all of the free AI tools mentioned previously. For each feature, you'll see a list of which of the popular tools offer these functionalities as of this book's writing.

LARGE LANGUAGE MODEL

All of the generative AI tools that leverage natural language processing have a large language model that allows them to work, but different tools run by different companies often use different models. If a generative AI program were a car, the "model" would be the engine that makes the whole thing work. And like car engines, different engines have different capabilities. The relative strengths of different "models" can also vary based on the data they were trained upon and their recency, as well as how they were trained and refined by their makers.

Like your smartphone apps in the app store, these models also are regularly updated to get better and better at what they do. For example, OpenAI's GPT model has versions GPT-3.5, GPT-3.5 Turbo, GPT-4, GPT-4o mini, GPT-4 Turbo, GPT-4o, and so on. Similarly, before Claude 3, there was Claude 2. Generally speaking, more recently developed models in a given model family (like GPT, Gemini, Claude, or Llama) will be more advanced and trained on more data (including recent data) than previous versions of the same model. If you have the choice between using either a more recent model or an older model and both options are free, then choosing the more recent model (like GPT-4o instead of GPT-4) is a no-brainer!

But for every rule, there are of course exceptions. OpenAI has a model called o1-preview on its premium plans. This model is different from other LLMs by ChatGPT and competitors in that before it responds to a request, it "reasons" through its response before delivering the final output to the user. This means a slower response time but it provides results that increase the level of "logic" in the output while decreasing the likelihood of hallucination. So in this way, o1 is a stronger model than GPT-4o, though at the time of its launch, o1 lacked the ability to work with the other functional extensions (like the ones we'll discuss and leverage in this book). Because at the time of this writing it lacks these additional functions (and because it is only available on premium plans), we won't focus on this model in this book.

When it comes to "what model is best," among the major players, it's a pretty tight race. So don't get too caught up in using the "right" ones! Find the ones you like and get excited for each new update!

WEB BROWSING

When a generative AI tool has web-browsing capabilities, this means that for answers to more recent queries, it can browse the web and use its natural language processing ability to summarize the information it finds. This enables these tools to find more recent information beyond the time frame of their training data cutoff, but it does not necessarily make them more likely to have completely accurate and hallucination-free results. When using these capabilities, I always recommend clicking through to the "source material" hyperlinked within the AI's answer to check both the credibility of the source it referenced and the validity of the summary the AI provided.

Despite having access to web browsing, most of the time, you will find that these models still rely first and foremost on their training data to answer your requests. So even tools that do not have the ability to browse the web might still be decent options. If you are looking for a summary of up-to-date information (say, from the past year), though, an AI with web browsing is very handy.

One note: These tools can (somewhat hilariously) "forget" that they have the ability to browse the web! If a tool with this capability tells you it cannot search the web, simply remind it that it can, and you'll soon have your answer complete with hyperlinks for further information.

- **Tools with web browsing:** ChatGPT Free (Limited, via GPT-4o), ChatGPT Plus, Microsoft Copilot (free and paid), Google Gemini (free and paid), Perplexity (free and paid), Meta AI (free)

VISION

Having "vision" functionality means that a user can upload an image into their AI chat, and the AI can "see" and "understand" the contents of the image. Combined with a text request, this capability can help you identify objects, transcribe handwritten text, and answer questions about the image.

- **Tools with vision functionality:** ChatGPT Free (Limited, via GPT-4o), ChatGPT Plus, Microsoft Copilot (free and paid), Google Gemini (free and paid), Claude (free and paid), Perplexity (paid only), Meta AI (free)

"CHAT WITH" DOCUMENTS FUNCTIONALITY

Attaching a PDF or text document to your chat can add a wealth of extra context to a given prompt, from providing a source of information from which to derive answers to training the AI on the contents of the document. With this feature, you can, for example, attach a long document like a contract or academic paper and ask the AI questions about it, or you can upload a sample of your writing to train the chat on your writing style. If your document is lengthy, you'll be best served by those tools with longer context windows, like the free version of Claude (200k context window on the Claude Sonnet model) or ChatGPT's GPT-4o (128k context window).

- **Tools allowing document attachment:** ChatGPT Free (Limited, via GPT-4o), ChatGPT Plus, Microsoft Copilot (free if using Microsoft Edge browser, or available in paid version with Microsoft 365), Google Gemini (paid only, with Google Drive), Claude (free and paid), Perplexity (free with a limit of three per day and paid)

AI IMAGE GENERATION

Many generative AI tools allow you to make incredible, fun, and inventive images in all sorts of artistic styles with just a text prompt (don't ask for images of public figures). This can be a fast and an easy way to both have fun and get creative, from creating beautiful or entertaining images with a prompt to inspiring your original art projects in the physical world.

- **Tools with AI image generation:** ChatGPT Free (Limited, via GPT-4o), ChatGPT Plus, Microsoft Copilot (free and paid), Google Gemini (free and paid), Perplexity (paid), Meta AI (free)

- **Other tools worth mentioning:** Two more popular and free-to-use text-to-image AI tools include Adobe Firefly (firefly.adobe.com) and Ideogram (ideaogram.ai). Ideogram is particularly skilled at including text in AI-generated images.

VOICE

"Voice" functionality allows you to talk out loud to the AI tool and get audible responses, as if you're having a natural conversation with a human. Basically, it works like a very, very skilled and personable Siri or Alexa. This tool can be great for when you need to be hands-free or if you are more of an auditory learner.

ChatGPT was the first of the AI tools mentioned in this book to offer this "Voice" functionality, but many tools have since jumped on the bandwagon. The tappable entry point for the "Voice" feature can vary across tools, but look for an icon to the right side of the "text entry" field in your chat. On ChatGPT, the icon will either look like headphones or a series of vertical lines (like a mini sound wave). In Meta AI, the symbol with three vertical lines opens the voice chat, and in Microsoft Copilot, the icon looks like a microphone (a vertical oval with a curved line surrounding its base).

- **Tools with voice functionality:** ChatGPT (Free and Paid), Meta AI (Free, via Facebook, Instagram, and WhatsApp messages), Microsoft Copilot (free and paid), Google Gemini (paid, via mobile app), Perplexity (via mobile app, paid with limited free access)

DATA ANALYSIS

ChatGPT stands out among the tools we've discussed for its data analysis feature available with GPT-4 and GPT-4o. With it, you can upload data in spreadsheet form, ask questions about the data, and with text prompts alone ask ChatGPT to summarize and visualize findings within the data, which it does leveraging a Python script that it runs calculations through. This feature also makes ChatGPT more skilled at complex mathematical equations, which is a noted weak point for most generative AI tools. The paid versions of Microsoft Copilot and Google Gemini can also help you accomplish data analysis tasks by asking questions about how to write formulas for or analyze your Excel file or Google Sheets.

- **Tools with data analysis:** ChatGPT Free (Limited, via GPT-4o), ChatGPT Plus, Microsoft Copilot (paid, with Microsoft 365), Google Gemini (paid, with Google Drive)

"CHAT WITH" YOUTUBE VIDEOS

A feature available on Google's Gemini is the ability to "chat with," summarize, and ask questions about lengthy YouTube videos by pasting in a link to the publicly available video with a request. This works with YouTube videos that have closed captions available. Perplexity AI can do a similarly strong job of summarizing YouTube videos or answering questions about their contents.

- **Tools to chat with and summarize YouTube videos:** Google Gemini (free and paid), Perplexity AI (free and paid)

CUSTOMIZABLE AI CHATBOTS OR "CUSTOM GPTS"

"Custom GPTs" are specialized versions of OpenAI's GPT model that are tailored to work for a specific purpose by paid users. ChatGPT Plus users can design their own custom GPTs by training them for a specific purpose through text prompts and attached documents, and even connecting them with other tools to perform additional actions. This allows even more flexibility and efficiency within ChatGPT, as instead of having to "retrain" a chat every time you want to do something specialized, you can instead call upon your pretrained custom GPT.

Better yet, if you *don't* want to spend time building your own custom GPTs, both ChatGPT Free users and ChatGPT Plus users can access the GPT Store, which is filled with over three million searchable custom GPTs made by others for you to use, though free users will have more limits on how much they can use these custom GPTs daily.

Recognizing the value of allowing users to train their own personalized chat experiences, other major players have followed OpenAI in developing features that let users make customizable chats. Examples include Claude's "Projects," Perplexity's "Spaces," Google Gemini's "Gems," and Meta's customizable "AI Characters" made with AI studio.

- **Tools with custom GPTS:** ChatGPT Free (Limited access to GPT Store), ChatGPT Plus (make customized GPTs and access GPT Store), Google Gemini (paid), Meta AI (free), Claude AI (paid), Perplexity AI (free and paid)

The Future of AI

These capabilities illustrate how generative AI tools can process inputs and generate content outputs in various formats, ranging from text to images to audio. The most popular tools will only continue to evolve and expand in their capabilities in new and exciting ways!

CHAPTER 2

Prompting 101

In the world of generative AI, you will hear the word *prompt* thrown around a lot. A prompt is just AI-speak for the instruction, input, or request given to an AI to achieve a specific output. A prompt can start a conversation, ask a question, give an instruction, and even create an image! A prompt can be short, like a simple question, or it can be lengthy and filled with complex context and directions. AI chats can also include more than one prompt, as you refine your request. Thus, prompts can also be considered just a part of the conversation—they are simply the inputs the human user puts in for the AI to converse with and respond to within your chat.

In this book, you'll be exposed to countless ways you can use AI tools to enhance your life, and you'll find thoroughly tested prompts that you could use as-is for some specific tasks. But the prompts in this book are by no means the be-all and end-all for prompting! Think of them instead as a jumping-off point to either edit and personalize or to inspire your chat conversations for ideas beyond the ones in this book!

Key Prompt Elements

Since the launch of OpenAI, many have joked that it is finally the time for English and communications majors to shine! When crafting a prompt, being able to write clearly can be immensely helpful in getting strong outputs. Ultimately, a strong output from an AI comes down to clear, specific communication in your prompt.

Having said that, don't worry if you're not the best writer. What's most important is to imagine you're seeking help from a person and explain your situation as clearly as you can. If you wanted to eat tacos for dinner, and you asked your partner to "Pick up some food at the store for dinner," you'd likely be disappointed with what they bring home. But if you told them, "I want to make chicken tacos for dinner. Could you go to the grocery store and pick up some chicken breasts, tortillas, sour cream, and shredded Mexican cheese? Don't buy salsa—we already have that at home," you'd be far more likely to get exactly what you want! A good prompt is very similar.

You'll find dozens of sample prewritten prompts in this book so you can get a sense of what works best. But there will be times when you need to write your own, so it helps to know how to craft a good request from scratch. Here are three key elements a successful initial prompt will have.

1. Specific Context

What contextual information will be helpful for the AI to know to inform its answer? Context can be brief or very detailed depending on what you need. Generally, the more specific and detailed your context, the more personalized an answer you will receive.

In our "taco" scenario, the specific context would be the "for dinner" part of the prompt. "For dinner" might imply to your partner that this meal includes them and your kids. If you said, "For your lunch," they might get a taco kit for one!

2. Specific Actions or Details

What action do you want the AI to take for you? Summarize? Teach? Create? Brainstorm? There are countless actions AI can assist with, and the words you choose to describe the action can result in a variety of different output structures.

In our taco scenario, the specific action is "Go to the grocery store and pick up ingredients." If you didn't specify "grocery store," your partner could reasonably decide to take a shortcut to Taco Bell. If you didn't say *not* to get salsa, they might have picked it up. Specific actions and details help!

3. The Goal or Ideal Output

What does success look like for your prompt? How might the output be structured and what special information might it contain? Why are you asking ChatGPT for help in the first place?

In our taco scenario, the goal is to be able to make chicken tacos. The ideal output requested from your partner is coming home with the right ingredients.

Develop Your Own Prompting Style

One final key takeaway: As conversational tools, LLMs will respond to *anything* you put into them (even if it's just "hello!"). You can always start simple. But the more specific you are in your prompts, the more relevant, robust, and personalized the AI-generated outputs will be—and the faster you'll get the results you seek. As you begin to work with AI tools, you will likely find your own way to communicate.

In the following sections, you'll learn keywords, directions, and tips that I've found useful for generating the best responses possible from AI tools.

Formatting Structure Possibilities

While not necessary for all prompts, you can request that the AI output is delivered in a particular form or style, from text to table charts to images and more. Throughout this book, you'll discover prompt examples for all kinds of formats. Some of these are detailed here for your reference with information on when each kind of format may be most helpful for your situation.

- **Plain text:** This is the standard way ChatGPT responds to most simple prompts or questions that do not otherwise ask for a particular structure for its output. It will typically consist of a series of paragraphs addressing your request, though ChatGPT may introduce its own formatting (i.e., any combo of the following text and formats) to help deliver the information. In many cases, not requesting a structure is just fine!

- **Conversational:** If you'd like ChatGPT to converse with you like a person, with shorter answers to your prompts instead of its typical lengthy responses, you may request in your prompt that it "use a short conversational response, like talking to a person." With this request, it will share tidbits of information at a time, and you can continually converse with it to ask follow-up questions. This output can be great for any kind of role-play scenario.

- **List:** For a brainstorming scenario, you can request the format in a "numbered list" or simply include a number in your prompt, like "Give me 15 ideas," and ChatGPT will automatically craft a numbered list. Another common scenario of a list is in how-tos; if you ask for a "step-by-step tutorial" or to "list the steps for how to ___," ChatGPT will respond with a clear numbered list of instructions.

- **Bullet-pointed summary:** Asking for a bullet-pointed summary of a topic will generally condense the length of ChatGPT's output significantly, which can be great for getting a lot of information more quickly or summarizing high-level takeaways. Requesting a specific number of bullet points to limit ChatGPT's answers can make your responses even tighter.

- **Guide:** If you are hoping to learn something new, a "guide" is a great structure to request in your prompt. Generally, these responses are longer but broken down into bolded sections and subsections that clearly outline a process or learning structure for the subject at hand.

- **Table or chart:** One of ChatGPT's more unique formats is the ability to chart out its answers in a table of sorted columns and rows. I've yet to see ChatGPT produce this format without it being specifically requested, so you have to ask for it. When requesting a table, you can ask simply for a "table that breaks down (category)," but for better results, it's a good idea to approach ChatGPT with an idea of what you'd like the "columns" in your table to be. One of the simplest tables is "Pros and Cons" for a particular subject, where one column is "Pros" and the other "Cons." Overall, tables can be a great way to compare things and organize information.

Beyond what's on this list, you might request any of the following: recipe, itinerary, outline, Q&A, lyrics, script, resume, syllabus, or template in your prompts. Even these are not all of the possible formats an output from AI can take, so don't be afraid to ask for other options and experiment.

Example Keywords and Verbs to Use

The words you use in your prompts can greatly influence how well ChatGPT's output matches your ultimate goal: The clearer and more specific your communication, the clearer and more specific the output! Think of it this way: If someone important asked you to teach them about a certain subject you are very knowledgeable about, how might the information you give them change if they requested a "brief overview" from you versus a "detailed analysis"? Those two requests would result in very different deliverables! The same is true for your AI prompting.

Following are some examples of adjectives and action verbs you could include in a prompt and guidance on how the choice of one word versus the other will adjust the response. Keep in mind, these are merely examples to help inspire you, not limit you! You really don't need a massive vocabulary to get value from AI, but a strong word choice can take your prompts and their resulting output to another level.

Action Verbs

- **Brainstorm:** For when you need a lot of ideas. Add a number for a specific amount!

- **Categorize:** For sorting items from a provided input based on their similarities.

- **Condense:** If the first response you get from AI is too long, you might say "condense your answer" in response. Adding the phrase "be concise" to your initial prompt can also significantly cut down on the length of its response.

- **Compare and Contrast:** Helpful when you are evaluating the merits of something.

- **Create or Make:** When you'd like AI to make something for you. For example: "Make an image" or "Create a guide."

- **Critique:** Helpful when you want constructive feedback on something.

- **Debate:** Engage in a debate with ChatGPT yourself, or have ChatGPT present arguments for and against a certain subject.

- **Draft:** Good for when you need the start of a piece of writing, like "draft an email."

- **Estimate:** Helpful if you are trying to get an approximate guess.

- **Explain:** Useful when you want to better understand a concept.

- **Justify:** For when you need help defending an idea, decision, or action.

- **Outline:** A great starting point when you're struggling with writer's block, need some guidance on structuring your work, or want a high-level summary.

- **Paraphrase:** Helpful for providing greater clarity on a complex topic.

- **Predict:** Get insight into what could happen in the future based on available context.

- **Role-Play:** When you'd like ChatGPT to pretend to be someone else when conversing with you.

- **Summarize:** Will deliver a shorter answer that is not overly detailed.

- **Templatize:** Useful for creating an easy-to-follow template with fill-in-the-blanks.

Adding descriptors to your prompts to emphasize the kind of output you would like to receive can adjust the length, tone, depth, and more. Here are some examples of powerful adjectives (and their opposites) to emphasize how adjectives in your prompts can adjust your responses.

Adjectives

- **Advanced vs. Elementary:** The first will result in a response that assumes you already have intermediate to advanced awareness of the topic. The second will give more of a basic overview.

- **Comprehensive vs. Concise:** The first will yield a longer, more thorough response, while the other will provide a shorter, higher-level summary.

- **Technical vs. Nontechnical:** The first may include jargon or an elaborate in-depth explanation of function, while the other will provide a result in layperson's terms.

Similarly, you can use adjectives in your prompt to describe the ideal tone and style of the writing ChatGPT produces for your output. ChatGPT's standard tone of voice for its responses tends to be neutral, professional, and friendly, and its style of writing aims to be clear and informative. Prompt it to change its tone, and it will adapt! For example, you could ask for something sarcastic or silly; Shakespearean or robotic. There's no limit to how the words you use in your prompt can alter your chat conversations to your liking.

Making the Most of Layers and Follow-Ups

Generative AI tools like ChatGPT are conversational, and therefore they work best when you work with them collaboratively. Your request doesn't have to be the "perfect prompt"—in fact, you will often be better off breaking your prompt into multiple steps. Why is this? You may notice that responses from AI chat tools, while they can be long, will not go on forever. So, if your initial prompt was to ask it to do 5 separate but related tasks, it may accomplish part of the task, but then stop. Or it may try to cram the whole response into a single response that contains everything, but not with the level of detail you might need or in the format that may be most helpful to you.

Instead, for complex tasks, you should aim to do what I call "prompt layering." (Though, for *all* tasks, regardless of their level of complexity, you can always ask more of AI as a follow-up in your conversation since it will recall what you have already discussed—so long as you remain with the same chat window.) In this book, you'll be introduced to a number of ways you can layer prompts to dive deeper and deeper into a subject or accomplish even more impressive tasks. Before we get to those specific ideas, here are a few universal follow-up prompts that you can leverage across conversations with ChatGPT.

- **"Give me more":** When asking ChatGPT to brainstorm a list of ideas, you'll generally want to request a specific number of ideas, like 10. If you'd like more examples, simply say "Give me more," and it will deliver another batch of ideas typically in the amount you originally requested.

- **"Tell me more about _____":** Learning about a new subject from ChatGPT? Ask it to dive deeper into a new phrase or topic it mentioned with this simple ask.

- **"Make this more _____":** Want to see the same response but in a slightly different tone, style, or length? Follow this phrase with any adjective of your choosing (like *inventive, sarcastic, detailed, condense,* etc.) and see what happens!

- **"Explain it to me like I'm 12":** When learning about a complex topic from ChatGPT, this response will alter its initial explanation into something more straightforward and accessible.

- **"Ask me 10 questions to better guide your response":** Having ChatGPT ask *you* questions can enable it to help you better solve very specific problems or deliver more personalized answers. Once the questions have been asked, respond and see how much it enhances ChatGPT's results.

- **"Based on our past conversation, if you were me, what else would you ask?":** Similarly, if you aren't sure what other prompts to give ChatGPT for the subject you are exploring, you can make that its responsibility instead. If a question it comes up with captures your attention, try sending that one next in your chat.

- **Ask for best practices ahead of the task:** We've established that giving ChatGPT clear and specific instructions and goals in your prompts results in better outputs. But what if you aren't aware of best practices for the task you are having ChatGPT assist you with? Before delivering your request to ChatGPT, a "pre-layer" you can leverage is asking ChatGPT to make a guide detailing best practices for the task you'll ultimately have it do. Then, in your next prompt, have it construct its output while keeping in mind the guide it previously created.

Prompting Shortcuts, Tips, and Tricks

Now that we've covered the basics of how to craft a good prompt, create better requests, and dive deeper into your conversations with generative AI, let's review some of my favorite tips and tricks to take your prompting from "good" to "great"!

Leverage Voice-to-Text Transcription

The voice-recording and transcription feature found within many AI chat tools is my favorite "hack" to use when prompting. You'll see it referenced quite a few times in this book! It can save you a *lot* of time on typing and therefore allow you to get more context to these tools much more quickly while further harnessing the conversational nature of these tools.

The mobile applications for the AI tools mentioned in this book all have this voice-to-text capability, whether baked into the app experience or connected to your phone's voice transcription functionality. Simply tap the "microphone" icon in the message field or on the bottom right of your smartphone's keyboard, and speak your prompt or thoughts out loud. Then send off your transcribed result as your prompt! By the way, if you want to try out any of the prompts in Part 2, reading them out loud into your AI tool of choice is a great way to test them out!

Provide an Example

A great way to add more context to your prompt and achieve an even better result is to include an example of what kind of output you are aiming for. For example, to get ChatGPT to respond with a certain writing style, add to the end of your prompt a copy + pasted example of some uncopyrighted writing you'd like it to emulate or attach a document that's written in the style or tone of voice you want. Want to create an AI-generated image inspired by a photo on your phone? Attach the photo for reference. Want it to structure its output just so? Write one sample section for it to emulate in its response. In your prompt, make sure it's clear where the example begins by saying something simple like "Use the example here" or "Use the attachment as inspiration."

Try Adding "Temperature"

One of the lesser-known prompting tips is adding a "temperature" to the end of your prompt when using any of the tools that leverage GPT models. Without getting overly technical, a temperature is a number from 0.0 to 1.0 that indicates to the model the degree of randomness or creativity it should use when generating an answer. Lower temperatures (closer to 0.0) will result in a more straightforward answer, clear and straight to the point, which is most valuable in endeavors that require more accuracy. A higher temperature (closer to 1.0) creates a more creative or diverse response and is a good option for brainstorming, storytelling, and other creative tasks.

If you don't add a temperature to your prompts, most ChatGPT responses tend to fall in the middle. To add temperature to your prompts, just say, for example: "temperature 0.1" or "temperature 0.9" at the end. Play around and see the difference!

Assign a Specific Role

You'll notice some of the prompts in this book begin with the assigning of a role to ChatGPT, like asking it to be "a personal nutritionist" or "a career coach specializing in the technology industry." This is because giving ChatGPT a certain "character" to play and perspective to consider in its response can give it further contextual insight. That way, it has a better sense of the type of answer you are looking to receive and can therefore become even more specialized or appropriate for your given ask.

Giving ChatGPT even more specific descriptors about the kind of person you would like it to "act as" can also be great for seeking unique perspectives from different types of individuals on a given topic or question or for just having a little fun with inventive role-play scenarios.

Add a Number

When seeking a number of items or ideas generated from ChatGPT, include an exact number of how many ideas or items you would like it to create. If you just ask for "an idea," it will give you one idea but likely with a lot of detail and justification backing it. If you ask for 40 ideas, you'll get a lengthy list, each with a very brief descriptor. Fifteen ideas? Somewhere in between. I like to start with 10 for most brainstorming scenarios. If you want more from there, you can always request more!

"Explain Your Thought Process"

Asking ChatGPT to "explain its thought process" or "take a deep breath" before answering more complex questions about strategy or logic has been shown to increase the quality of its results by recent studies done by Google DeepMind researchers.

Another benefit? When the AI explains its thought process, you can learn how to follow a similar thought process in the future, or, alternatively, you can play devil's advocate, asking follow-up questions to pick apart its thought process and get clearer justification on its suggestions.

Experiment with Custom Instructions

When using ChatGPT specifically, you can leverage a feature called "Custom Instructions" to save time on prompting ChatGPT with the same context every time you start a new chat. Think of it as the ultimate prompt layer—a universal set of instructions and context for ChatGPT to keep in mind whenever you use it. To add or update your instructions, click on your username, then "Personalization," then "Customize ChatGPT." Here, you can enter extra information about yourself to help ChatGPT provide you with better, more personalized responses, as well as instructions for how you prefer ChatGPT to respond to you, like "I like straightforward explanations and learn well with analogies" or "When I say 'my business,' I'm referring to my side hustle where I sell decorated party cookies on Etsy."

Commit Material to "Memory"

ChatGPT also has a feature called "Memory," which effectively stores helpful nuggets of information about you from your chats so that it can use them as helpful additional context in future conversations. You can control whether the feature is turned on through a toggle in your settings, and see what "Memories" are stored there as well. Just tap your username, then "Personalization," then "Manage Memory." Additionally, when you are chatting with ChatGPT and you'd like it to add something specific to your "Memory" (like something you'd always like to keep in mind when you are having it help you plan a vacation), simply say "Commit this to memory" and it will!

Course Correcting and Feedback

When trying generative AI tools like ChatGPT for the first time, many people grow frustrated if it doesn't work the way they expected it to. But like any other skill, it takes practice. Plus, remember that these tools have context memory and are highly adaptable. Here are some proven ways to course-correct the AI if its initial response is not quite what you were looking for.

- **Stop the response if necessary:** When you submit your prompt, you'll see a square "stop" button appear in the chat bar from which you sent your message. If you can tell the response is already not quite what you are looking for, you can stop the generation by tapping this before providing additional feedback.

- **Provide feedback:** Like you would with a person who didn't quite understand the original assignment, in your subsequent prompt to ChatGPT, provide feedback so that it can course-correct. What did you like about its previous response? What would you like it to change in the next attempt?

- **Use affirmatives over negatives:** Generally speaking, while these tools are designed to interpret context regardless of how they are written, try to phrase your feedback and prompts in the affirmative ("do") rather than negative ("don'ts"). Affirmative prompts tend to be a little clearer and more direct, and negations might add unnecessary complexity, leading to confusion especially if used in complex sentences or very long prompts.

- **Remind the tool of its capabilities:** Believe it or not, AIs will sometimes forget what they are capable of. For example, while many of these tools have the ability to browse the web for more recent answers, their official training data cuts off at a certain point in time. When you ask the tool to summarize popular news headlines from the past month, you may be met with an apology, saying its training data was cut off a year prior. But you *know* this tool can search the web! Simply remind it: "You do have the ability to browse the web: use your web-browsing feature to accomplish this." With this reminder, the tools that do have this will generally adjust right away. You'll know if you've been successful if a clickable hyperlink appears in its response.

- **Don't rely on "try again":** Most of these generative AI tools have a "try again" or "regenerate" button (it looks like a circular arrow) that appears just beneath its response. When this button is selected, the original response is entirely erased, and the tool will proceed to answer your same original prompt but in a slightly different way, like with a different structure. This is my least favorite functionality because it allows users to forget that these tools are conversational. Also, because no additional feedback or instructions are given, the next response will likely not be much better.

Organizing Your Chat Histories

For most of the AI tools in this book, every time you go to the tool in your web browser or within your mobile app, you'll find a new, blank chat window waiting for you to put in your first prompt. Starting a new chat is generally beneficial if you are looking to do something new within your AI tool because this allows you to start fresh and not be concerned about the tool incorporating unrelated instructions from previous chats. Put another way, that context memory you learned about earlier? It is limited to the context of any individual chat.

But what if you want to pick up where you left off or return to an old chat from days ago? Instead of re-prompting this new chat with all the context from the last time, simply open up the history of your chats and find the recent chat you are looking for. If after using these tools you start to use them as frequently as I do (which is to say, *a lot*), here are some helpful tips on keeping your chat history clean and organized.

- **Rename your chats:** Generative AI tools where you can start new chats will assign your chat a name automatically, but sometimes the particular label can be hard to find for future reference. In your chat history or "recent" chats, hover over your chat name or look for three dots (...) or a carrot (v) symbol that appears near the chat name, then click the option to "rename" or "edit" the chat. Other tools allow editing when you click on or long press the name of the chat directly.

☐ **Possible with:** ChatGPT, Google Gemini, Claude, Perplexity, Meta AI (browser)

- **Archive or delete your histories:** Deleting or archiving chats you do not anticipate returning to in the future will make it easier for you to find those that are most important to you. Click those same three dots (...) when hovering over a chat and select "trash can" to permanently delete that chat. Or, in ChatGPT, you can archive the chat instead. This will allow you to find it again within your ChatGPT settings should you change your mind and want to return to it again.

☐ **Possible with:** ChatGPT, Google Gemini, Claude, Perplexity, Meta AI (browser)

- **Search for your past chats:** The easiest way to find an old chat? Search for it! ChatGPT, Claude, and Perplexity all allow you to search through your past chats for specific keywords that may have been within them so you can dig up your treasures from past chats. Just find your chat history and list of recent threads in your app of choice and look for a "magnifying glass" icon.

☐ **Possible with:** ChatGPT, Claude, Perplexity

- **Pin or favorite your favorite chats:** Gemini, Claude, and Perplexity all have easy ways for you to keep your most important chats top of mind. When in Gemini on your web browser, click the three dots next to your chat's name and "pin" the chat so it always remains at the top of your chat history. By long pressing on the chat name in the mobile app, you can do the same. On your web browser when using Claude, look for a "star" symbol in the top right of the chat to favorite the chat. Finally, in Perplexity, you can add multiple chats on similar topics to a "Space" or "Collection" so they are easily found together as you continue work on a particular project.

☐ **Possible with:** Google Gemini, Claude, Perplexity

- **Share your chats with others:** If you are using AI to help someone else find answers or solutions, many tools allow you to share the full chat history with them to pick up where you left off and see all you have already done in that chat. In ChatGPT, hover over the chat name and select the three dots that appear (or long press the chat name on mobile), and then select "share." In Perplexity, look for a "share" button in the top right of the chat on mobile or web. In Gemini, select a share symbol resembling a "less than" sign, click "share," and choose "Entire chat." These actions will all create a link to the specific chat you have chosen to share. When the person you have shared the link with continues the chat, you won't see their conversations. Likewise, if you continue the chat yourself, they cannot see your subsequent chats. With Gemini and Meta AI (browser), you have the ability to specifically share just the response and the prompt preceding it with someone else. In Gemini, just select the same symbol, "share," and "This prompt & response." In Meta AI, click the icon to the right of your response that looks like a paper airplane, then "copy link."
  □ **Possible with:** ChatGPT, Perplexity, Google Gemini, and Meta AI (browser)

The Power of Chat Histories

Keeping a well-organized chat history can help you more easily return to all of the valuable creations and discoveries you will make and learn through your interactions with your AI tools. So whether you are picking up your AI-guided French lessons, refreshing your memory of your trip itinerary, or checking in with your AI career coach, you can jump back in even faster!

— PART 2 —

Using AI to Improve Your Life

Welcome to Part 2! This is where the fun really begins. You'll find eight chapters themed around categories that explore countless ways AI can make your daily life more productive, inspiring, easy, and fun! From the kitchen to the job search, healthy New Year's resolutions to incredible vacations, and your relationship with yourself to your relationships with others, you'll discover how to leverage AI in unique and clever ways to achieve your goals, save time, and level up your life.

Each chapter includes both multistep prompts and simpler, shorter ideas. The multistep prompts illustrate how to leverage layering to achieve the most impactful results or use the same chat for related topics, thanks to AI's context memory. The shorter ideas (which appear at the end of each chapter) cover a variety of other examples related to the theme that will generate great results with a single prompt.

Every idea in this book contains example prompts that I wrote and tested for optimal results to guide your understanding. (These prompts appear indented in this font.) Think of them as templates that you might fill in with your own personal details when the time comes. Please keep in mind, though, that these prompts are not just templates—they are meant to be inspiration. You need not use these exact words in the exact order to get great results with AI. By pairing these examples with the prompting theory you learned in Part 1, you'll soon be using AI with incredible prompts of your own!

You'll notice in this part that the terms *ChatGPT* and *AI* are mentioned interchangeably. As mentioned in Part 1, there are many free AI tools that can be leveraged for all of the scenarios in this book. I use *ChatGPT* because it is the most recognizable name for a generative AI tool.

One final tip! One of the best ways to experience this part of the book is to see for yourself the power of AI as you explore these use cases, as they're called. I recommend downloading any of the free AI apps discussed in Part 1 to your smartphone (my personal favorite? ChatGPT!) and trying out the prompts by just reading them out loud right from the book. Skip the typing and tap the "microphone" icon in the apps or on your keyboard. Then just read the example prompt aloud, send it off, and see the results for yourself!

CHAPTER 3

Home Life

S ince most of the buzz around AI tools is about revolutionizing work and industries, you may not realize the massive impact these tools can have right in your own home. Many people already understand the benefits of having home assistants like Google Home or Alexa at the ready. But if you are not interested in an "always listening" device, ChatGPT can be a similarly excellent assistant, while also providing you with more robust details and answers.

In this chapter, you'll discover many ways to use AI tools to cut down on the tedium of domestic tasks, improve your life, and even save you money. You'll be inspired to organize and declutter with clear personalized plans and discover inventive ways to decorate your home and take care of your lawn. You'll learn to prompt ChatGPT through understanding the nuances of your home appliances, diagnosing problems, and evaluating solutions. You'll even discover how to get ChatGPT's guidance on the nitty-gritty of home and vehicle maintenance, deep cleaning, and preparing your home for a new family member's arrival.

With fast answers, deep insights, and creative responses, ChatGPT will make your everyday home tasks more efficient and more enjoyable. As you begin to use them, you will undoubtedly find new ways to leverage AI tools at home!

DECLUTTER YOUR HOME

How AI Can Help You Declutter Your Home

No matter the size of your home, if you aren't a naturally organized and tidy person, the prospect of cleaning your living space up and out can be a daunting one. There are so many rooms to consider, drawers and closets stuffed with items you haven't thought about in years, along with countless items that you've held on to for far too long but have always had trouble parting with.

From creating a home organization checklist with time frames to providing you with behavioral strategies to help you let go of what's holding your tidy-space dreams back, ChatGPT can aid in making the whole process more efficient and effective.

Set Up Your Initial Request

For the best results, include in your prompt specifics on the spaces you are focusing on, the amount of time you can commit to your organization project, the date/time by which you'd like to reach your goal, and any challenges that have held you back in the past. For this scenario and others like it, asking for a "checklist" specifically is usually the most helpful prompt so that ChatGPT will create a clear breakdown of specific things to do and an order in which to do them.

Sample Starter Prompt

Make a robust checklist for organizing and decluttering my home, considering all potential areas (drawers, surfaces, closets, etc.) that could contain clutter in each of the spaces. I am focused solely on organization and getting rid of items. Deep cleaning is not of interest at this time. These are the spaces I would like to focus on:

- Main bedroom, bathroom, and closet
- My adult children's childhood bedrooms
- Hall closet
- Kitchen pantry
- Garage

In your list, assign time-bound suggestions for each activity, allocated according to the expected effort of each task, so that I can plan to dedicate that specific amount of time to that one task over the next 2 months.

Additional Ways to Personalize

Break Down Your To-Dos Room by Room

Breaking down larger tasks into smaller, more manageable tasks is a proven way to help tackle procrastination and maintain motivation. Once you've generated your first checklist, you can have your AI tool of choice make a further breakdown of your checklist for each room in your home.

Make an even more detailed checklist with tips and tricks for the main bedroom specifically.

Address Sentimentality

A big part of what makes cleaning and decluttering difficult is the sentimental attachment you can have to objects in your household. Giving meaningful items away or trashing them can be very tough. ChatGPT can be an empathetic but also practical assistant in guiding you through the process while providing you with strategies to get rid of unnecessary clutter and talk to others in your life about doing this as well.

I'm struggling with deciding what to do with my adult children's items that are still at my house. I feel sentimental toward a lot of them, and for the other items, I'm not sure I have the right to get rid of them. Give me a strategy for approaching this situation with my children and how to handle my holdups.

Get Guidelines for Decluttering

Another way ChatGPT can help in your home decluttering project is by creating a set of guidelines for you to follow as you tackle different areas of your home. These frameworks can be excellent fallbacks when you find yourself struggling with what to do with an item. In this prompt, include details on your ultimate goal and an understanding of how much you are really hoping to get rid of.

Help me come up with a list of 5 questions to ask myself when I am cleaning out my closet to determine whether I should keep an item of clothing.

DEEP CLEAN YOUR HOME

How AI Can Help You Deep Clean Your Home

Maintaining a pristine home can be a daunting task, but the joy of having a well-cared-for space is worth it! Still, if you're new to the concept of deep cleaning, let ChatGPT create a complete room-by-room plan for committing to a cleaner home. You can also ask it to sort by the frequency with which you should perform each task to create stronger cleaning habits and practices throughout the year.

Set Up Your Initial Request

Start by requesting that ChatGPT make a basic schedule for maintaining a clean home, detailing the recommended frequency for cleaning various spaces and appliances around your home. While you *could* list out every room in your home within this initial prompt, doing so may create a less detailed guide, as ChatGPT may condense its response so that it can fit at least some information for each requested room. Instead, the sample prompt here will establish a strong start for future layers.

I want to be better about regularly cleaning my home and home appliances according to strategies recognized by home cleaning experts. Please create a systematic deep-cleaning checklist sorted by the frequency it should occur (weekly, biweekly, monthly, biannually, annually, etc.) and by room in the house.

Additional Ways to Personalize ──•

Request Additional Rooms

The output of the sample prompt will include details for all rooms commonly found in the home (kitchen, bedrooms, bathroom, living room, etc.), but you can follow it with another prompt layer to be sure it matches your home. Try asking for a similar schedule for specific rooms to personalize the results even further.

Following this structure, create an even more detailed guide specifically for my kitchen, mudroom, and laundry room.

Get Detailed Tips and Tricks for Each Task

Once you have a detailed guide for specific rooms in your house, you can ask for additional instructions on best practices for performing each task on your cleaning list. Because of AI's context window, you can reference details further back in your chat to elaborate on. Since you've already established a clean structure for your prompt, the subsequent instructions will follow a similar pattern.

Now for each task on the list, provide me with clear instructions, tips, or little-known strategies for performing the tasks efficiently and effectively. Start with all tasks for the kitchen.

Learn to Make DIY Natural Alternatives to Cleaning Chemicals

Whether you are hoping to avoid certain chemicals or looking to save money with homemade alternatives, creating your own natural cleaners at home can help. Instead of sorting through the results of multiple online searches for alternatives to all the different cleaning products available, ChatGPT can create a comprehensive guide to common cleaners and recipes with DIY natural alternatives, and it can even provide insight into the expected impact on your wallet.

> Please provide me with 10 common household cleaning supplies that contain chemicals, then a recipe for each cleaner on how to make a natural alternative. For each alternative, explain how effective the natural alternative is compared to the chemical cleaner. Finally, provide an estimate of the cost difference of one approach versus the other. Explain your thinking.

MAINTAIN YOUR HOME

How AI Can Help You Maintain Your Home

Regularly maintaining your home is essential to preserving its value, preventing costly repairs, and even saving money in the long term through maintenance practices that boost energy efficiency. But it can be really difficult to remember all the best practices for maintaining your home. With ChatGPT's help, you can create a complete checklist for regular home maintenance tasks and receive instructions on how to accomplish them.

Set Up Your Initial Request

Many new homeowners simply don't know what they don't know. It's not like most schools teach the ins and outs of caring for AC units or clearing dryer vents! If you are starting from square one, ChatGPT can help by making you a basic beginner's guide to regular home maintenance. Once you have this, you'll have a better understanding of what specifics to ask in future prompts.

Sample Starter Prompt

I am new to home ownership and need your assistance in creating a robust checklist of all essential home maintenance tasks. In this guide, please include details on what needs to be done, at what frequency, and the reason why it is important to do.

Additional Ways to Personalize

Get Specific Guidance for Your Home

Your starting prompt will provide you with general home maintenance tips that all homeowners should consider. But the year in which your home was built, its location, and its style can also impact the specifics of its maintenance. By providing this added detail in your next prompt, you can get an even deeper understanding of any maintenance nuances to consider for your home in particular that might not apply to homes built in other decades or areas.

My home is located in Atlanta, Georgia, and was originally built in the 1950s. Please add to your guide any other maintenance tasks or considerations I should keep in mind based on the age and location of my home.

Understand and Budget for Maintenance Costs over Time

As most homeowners know, the cost of home ownership stretches far beyond the mortgage payment. There are maintenance costs to consider, both for your home and larger appliances within it, as well as monthly utility bills and unexpected costs that result from things that might be preventable with a little extra forethought. If you are looking to find ways to save on these extra costs, this prompt can provide you with a robust guide to use as a starting point. From there, asking for more detail and follow-up questions can lead you to actionable tasks that will help you save on the extra costs of home ownership.

Create a comprehensive guide to saving money or preventing unexpected costs as a homeowner, including details on maintenance activities to ensure cost savings in the long run, how to improve the longevity of expensive household appliances, and how to save on bills during different seasons of the year.

Weigh the Merits of Cost-Saving Tasks for Your Home

It can be valuable to use this follow-up prompt to understand what actions might result in the best "bang for your buck" so you know what actions to focus on first.

For each recommendation above, please estimate how much money the action will cost how much money it will save in the long term. Explain your thinking.

Initially Diagnose Concerns with Appliances

Hearing odd noises from your appliances can be unsettling, especially if you have recently moved or are a first-time homeowner. Similarly, when things around your home stop working as expected or you see an "error" indicator or a red light, it can be deeply frustrating. Instead of immediately looking up the home warranty or calling a specialist, ChatGPT can help diagnose the issue and recommend solutions or necessary next steps, while putting your mind at ease.

I have been hearing a lot of bumps and creaks in the night in my home. We recently moved in, and this house was built in the 1960s, then flipped. It's been really cold recently, and I'm also starting to notice small cracks appearing in the paint on our walls and I'm really concerned. What could be going on, and do I need to be concerned or call a specialist?

We just installed a new LG Dryer. However, we've noticed that midway through the drying cycles the dryer has been stopping. The display is showing "d80." What does this mean, what might be causing the dryer to stop, and what could we do to fix the issue?

CREATE A FAMILY CHORE SYSTEM

How AI Can Help You Implement Family Chores

If you are a parent with a seemingly never-ending list of tasks, you might consider sharing that work with your children. Assigning household chores to your children can lighten your mental load, and it can also help your children build strong habits that last a lifetime. ChatGPT can not only inspire you with inventive and fun ways to introduce these new systems to your household; it can also recommend age-appropriate tasks and incentive systems while suggesting fairly distributed assignments among your family.

Set Up Your Initial Request

If your family is totally new to chores systems, you may want to use your first prompt to uncover different approaches to a chores system you are interested in trying. Include details on the makeup of your family so that this information can be leveraged to inform subsequent prompts. Other things you might include in this prompt are requesting a pros/cons breakdown of each suggested method.

Sample Starter Prompt

I would like to implement a chores system with our family to lighten the burden of household tasks on my husband and me, while also teaching my children (ages 7 and 10) more responsibility. Please suggest different methods families use for successfully introducing and implementing household chores in their family, including incentives and accountability/ enforcing methods.

Brainstorm a List of Possible Chores

Now that you've gotten inspired by different ways you might implement new chores systems for your family, you can enlist AI's help with brainstorming chores that your children may be able to assist with. Include what chores you *know* you'd like help with, but also request that AI help you come up with other possible tasks that you may not be thinking of, including some that may be less frequent, like those that need to happen monthly.

> I need your help coming up with and sorting a list of possible household chores that I may be able to assign to my children, keeping in mind their ages. Off the top of my head, I believe they can help with caring for our pet cat and cleaning up and taking care of their bedrooms and themselves (teeth brushing, bathing, etc.) without me having to nag them. Please make a complete list of other things they could potentially help with around the home, sorted by frequency.

Determine Age-Appropriate Chores

Now that you've got a great list of all of the possible things your children could assist you with (which you can refine or increase to your heart's content with any additional follow-up prompts in your conversation), you can leverage ChatGPT to help you determine which items on the list are appropriate for each age. This can be a great starting point for helping to off-load the work while also promoting the development of habits that can reasonably stick, by assigning responsibilities that are within the capabilities of your younger children.

> I'm trying to determine what chores are age-appropriate for my kids. Given the list of chores you have just listed out, please suggest which tasks are appropriate for my 7-year-old, for my 10-year-old, for both, or for neither without parental supervision. The output should be a table, where the rows are the chore type, and the columns are "Chore," "Frequency" (Daily/Weekly/Monthly)," and "Appropriate for (Both, Age 10, With Supervision)."

Assign a Chore Schedule

Now that you've got all your chores sorted and categorized, you can leverage ChatGPT to help you quickly make a balanced distribution of tasks to be done among your kids in the form of an easy chart that you can replicate for a board at home. Detail in your prompts any chores you'd like all of your kids to do, then request that all remaining activities be fairly distributed. By requesting that ChatGPT estimate the time to accomplish the chore, you can more easily vet how equitable the distribution is.

I have decided I'd like both of my kids to do the following chores on a daily basis <list the chores> and the following on a weekly basis <list the chores>. Please evenly divide all of the remaining "Weekly" or "Monthly" chores between my 7- and 10-year-old, while keeping assigned tasks appropriate for their respective ages. Then, make 2 separate tables that are the chore charts for my 10-year-old and my 7-year-old. Each row in the table should be the assigned chore. The columns should be "Chore Name," "Frequency" (Daily, Weekly, or Monthly)," and the expected amount of time each task might take.

Suggest Creative Incentivization Strategies

Now that you've designed your chores system, you could use ChatGPT to seek inspiration for creative ways to introduce this new process to your kids and to incentivize them to adopt and maintain it. Whether it's determining a weekly allowance (within your family's budget), or suggesting nonmonetary ways to instill excitement around completing household responsibilities, ChatGPT can be an excellent partner in making housework shared work.

We've decided we do not want to compensate chores in our house with money. However, we still want to provide fun incentives to encourage our kids to adopt and maintain these new assignments. Please suggest 5 unique incentive strategies we could implement and explain your thought process for each recommendation.

PLAN HOME IMPROVEMENT PROJECTS

How AI Can Help with Home Renovations

If you are considering a home renovation, you likely already know you are in for a lot of work and stress…but that the payoff will be sweet! For first-time renovators, AI can help you get a clear understanding of what to expect for projects you are committed to or even vaguely considering, from cost and time estimates to the details on the overall process and how to approach hiring contractors. Even if you've got a few renovations under your belt, AI can also serve as a fun and inspirational partner, helping to bring the image in your head to life, or discovering new inventive ways to approach the challenge.

Set Up Your Initial Request

In your prompt, be as descriptive as possible about the home project you have in mind. What exactly are you hoping to change? In what city or state are you doing the renovation (to help estimate the cost of labor/parts)? If you are redoing a particular room, what is the square footage? Asking for low, medium, and high estimates will give you a good sense of the rough minimum and maximum you might expect to pay for each component of your project so that you can quickly ground your expectations and better prioritize what are "must haves" and "nice to haves."

Sample Starter Prompt

I'm hoping to do a significant renovation of my bathroom to make it more modern, but I'm trying to get a better estimate of the potential costs. This renovation would involve replacing my Jack and Jill–style sinks from the 1970s with a more modern set with nice cabinetry; replacing the tile throughout with new tile; removing the porcelain tub and replacing it with a larger, more luxurious freestanding tub; redoing the shower entirely to give it more square footage; and replacing the toilet as well as all lighting fixtures. The room is about 150 square feet. Please break down robust high/medium/low estimates of the potential costs of this renovation, given that I live in Wilmington, Vermont, and the renovation will be done in 2025.

Additional Ways to Personalize

Get Expectations on Timing

Once you have a clearer idea of the costs associated with your project, you may be wondering, "Okay, but how long is this going to take?" In your next prompt, enlist ChatGPT's aid by having it make three similar estimates for the same project. By asking it to clarify its assumptions and break down more details on what could lead to unexpected delays, you can get a better understanding of the potential longest time commitment.

For the same project described above, please make low/medium/high estimates for the amount of time in weeks the project may likely take. Clarify the assumptions for your estimates. Finally, detail what elements of the project are more likely to take longer than expected, and why.

Make a Step-by-Step Plan

If only you could dive right into your renovation process after the idea inspires you! Unfortunately, there are a lot of small steps along the way. If this is your first experience with a major renovation project, ChatGPT can create a straightforward guide on how to approach your renovation and in what order, and provide any advice you subsequently ask for during each step as well.

Please create a step-by-step guide of all the things I must do, as the one desiring the home renovation, before any of the renovations actually begin. For each step, provide tried-and-true advice in addition to little-known tips to ensure the most successful and efficient process possible for me.

Inspire Your Home Design

AI tools with image-generation capabilities can be wonderful collaborative partners when designing a vision board for yourself or when working with a designer to help you communicate the vision in your head and bring it to life. Detail the elements, style, or even color palettes of your desired new room, then request your AI tool to make a visual of what it might look like. You can get very detailed (as if to visualize your clear vision) or let AI take the reins with a little less guidance so that you can explore different styles. After AI has made its first image, you can prompt it again for different inspiration while specifying what elements to maintain. Repeat or refine to your heart's content!

Make an image of a sleek and modern bathroom featuring the following key elements: a standing glass shower, a stand-alone luxurious tub, a double sink with mirror and cabinets, a modern toilet, and a tile floor. This is to act as design inspiration for my renovation.

(Second Prompt) Please do another take on a modern bathroom that fits the needs described before but has a different color/style/lighting from what you've just done.

Get Guidance on Contractor Hiring

Now that you've got a solid understanding of expected costs, timing, to-dos, and what you want, it's time to kick off the search for the people who can help you make your renovation dreams a reality. If this is your first time undergoing this process, ChatGPT can help guide you along the way with tips on how to effectively source, hire, and even negotiate with varied contractors.

For my project, I will need to hire a number of contractors. Please provide a guide with expert tips on finding, evaluating, negotiating with, and hiring contractors. Include suggestions for how to find great contractors to work with, pertinent questions I should ask, and how to find a fair price for the work so that I avoid overpaying.

MAINTAIN YOUR CAR

How AI Can Help with Car Maintenance

Regularly maintaining your car not only increases your safety in your vehicle; it also adds a significant amount of time to your vehicle's lifespan (or will lead to greater resale value in the future) compared to doing nothing at all. Still, many people who own their cars do not have extensive automotive knowledge and may avoid car maintenance for fear of being taken advantage of via unnecessary or unfairly priced repairs. Understanding the best practices in car maintenance is essential for successful vehicle ownership, as is evaluating the purchase of a used vehicle.

Artificial intelligence can help bridge any knowledge gap you have, creating a detailed checklist of considerations for regular maintenance while also guiding you to a decision on whether different maintenance tasks should be done immediately or if any can wait, especially if you are on a tighter budget.

Set Up Your Initial Request

Start by requesting a basic checklist of what you should be doing and how frequently. In your prompt, include specifics like details on the mileage of the car in question or its current general condition to make your response even more personalized. If you have a history of maintenance that you can recall, it can be helpful to include that context as well.

Sample Starter Prompt

I purchased a used car about 3 years ago but have done very little to maintain it outside of the occasional oil change. It has 50,000 total miles. I know I should be doing more to maintain it, but I have very little knowledge on the subject. Make a robust checklist, organized by the frequency at which they should occur, of all maintenance tasks I should be doing to increase the longevity of my car.

Get Specifics for the Year and Model of Your Car

The preceding prompt will likely give you a thorough but generic guide to best practices for caring for a car. By following up and asking for specific guidance as they relate to your year and model of car, you may uncover new considerations that are specifically useful for you to know about maintaining your car.

> Is there anything else to consider specifically for a car based on its model and year? It is a 2019 Ford Taurus.

Determine What May Most Urgently Need Attention

If, as in the example prompt, it has been a long while since your car was last looked at, ChatGPT can give you recommendations for the types of maintenance work you might want to consider first, or what you might reasonably expect to hear from a mechanic when you do take your car in. It can even give you a rough idea of the range of costs you might expect to pay for such maintenance work.

> Point out any important or more urgent maintenance actions that I should consider given the mileage on my car. Please also roughly estimate the expected cost for this kind of car maintenance, accounting for parts and labor.

Understand How to Evaluate Maintenance Recommendations

Sometimes you take your car in for an innocent check-up and end up getting a laundry list of repairs that you weren't expecting. If these repairs fall outside your budget or you don't feel comfortable enough with cars to ask the right questions, this information can be overwhelming. With ChatGPT's help, you can understand what typical maintenance practices look like and even generate follow-up questions to ask your regular mechanic (or a second-opinion mechanic) to ensure you are getting just the work you *need* done at a fair price.

I recently took my car in to be maintained at the dealership, and they gave me a list of about $4,000 in suggested maintenance tasks for my car. I worry they aren't recommending just "must haves" but also "nice to haves." For each item on the list, explain best practices for frequency of maintenance, why it is important, and what questions I might ask the dealer or a second-opinion mechanic on the relative necessity of all repairs. Here are all the items on their repair list: timing belt replacement, fluid flush (transmission, coolant, power steering), and strut and shock replacements. Please also let me know if those price points sound in range with what would be expected.

Better Evaluate a Used Car for Purchase

Buying a used car is often a more economical choice than buying a car right off the lot, and if the car has been well maintained, it can also be a great deal! But if you don't know much about cars and what questions you should ask, you could end up getting a *lousy* deal. AI can guide you through the process, providing suggestions on what to ask for and what to do to better understand the condition of the car you are considering purchasing.

I am thinking about purchasing a 2015 Honda Pilot with 84,000 miles. The exterior looks great, but I want to make sure I have a full understanding of how it has been maintained by its owner thus far before buying. What questions should I ask the owner before making my final purchase? Is there anything I can do myself to verify the car is still in good shape?

SUGGEST HOME DECOR USING PICTURES OF YOUR SPACE

Need inspiration for redecorating a room in your home? AI can provide suggestions and even generate images for a new look for your space. Snap a photo of your current space to upload and provide some details about what your goals and dreams may be for this room while giving information about the room's rough layout and size. Ask your AI tool to act as an interior designer to provide critique and, if you'd like, request it to create an image for design inspiration.

> Attached is an image of my home office (8 feet by 13 feet) that I need design advice for. My goal is to have a functional, tidy, sleek, and modern-looking space for work. Acting as an interior designer, tell me what is and is not working about the room's current design and layout and suggest improvements. Finally, generate an image to inspire a new approach.

CREATE A PLAN TO MAINTAIN HOME ORGANIZATION HABITS

If you have successfully downsized and organized your home, congratulations! Much of the most difficult work has been completed. Still, it is important to not forget the work that comes after—the effort to maintain your new space, stick to your new habits, and avoid having to start the whole process over again in a few years. ChatGPT can help guide you through a reflection process on your past habits and suggest strategies to maintain your home after your recent accomplishments.

> After decluttering, I want to avoid reverting to old habits. First, ask me 10 questions that I can answer to help you determine what kinds of behavior and thought patterns lead me to create clutter. After I have answered your questions, you should then give me 10 strategies or little-known tips for maintaining the cleanliness and organization of my home long term, catered to what you've learned about me.

CARE FOR INDOOR PLANTS

Keeping plants indoors can have numerous benefits while also presenting many challenges. They can lift spirits; enhance air quality; be the focus of an excellent hobby; and, of course, add a nice aesthetic appeal to a home—but they can also be tricky to care for if you haven't yet acquired your "green thumb." ChatGPT can advise you on how to care for your plant collection by answering questions about how to care for certain plants or even diagnosing issues with your plant based on a description or uploaded photos.

> Here is a picture of my *Begonia maculata*. I'm concerned that the tips of the leaves are becoming brown and dry. Please tell me what you think could be happening and ask me any questions that would help you better diagnose the issue and provide a recommendation for the issue.

PROVIDE GUIDANCE ON GARDEN WILDLIFE

Whether you are developing a gardening hobby or you want to take better care of your lawn, ChatGPT can provide tips on everything from how to deter unwelcome pests to how to attract welcome wildlife like honeybees, monarch butterflies, and more to support a healthy ecosystem. It can even provide tips on reducing or completely avoiding pesticides or chemicals in your gardening practices.

> I have recently started a garden in my backyard, and I love it! Unfortunately, the wildlife nearby (deer, rabbits, raccoons) does too. How can I deter the wildlife from eating from my garden without harming them? Create a robust guide for deterring each animal I mentioned.

PREPARE YOUR HOME FOR A NEW PET

Welcoming a new pet into your home can be exciting, but it can also produce its fair share of anxiety. Many adjustments generally need to be made to keep your new housemate safe and make sure they can adjust with ease. ChatGPT can offer guidance as you prepare for these changes, making sure critical details are not missed so you can rest easy as you adjust to your new living situation. Keep in mind, a similar prompt could be used for the arrival of a new baby or an elderly relative moving in for long-term care.

My family is adopting our first kitten. Craft me a detailed and well-organized guide on how to best prepare our home for the kitten to make sure that it is kept from harm or accidents. This guide should only include specific details to do with our home space and also include details on protecting our home and furniture from damage from the new kitten.

FIX ISSUES AROUND THE HOME

Leaky faucet? Clogged drain? Running toilet? Gaps in the caulk in your tiles? A lot of issues at home can be easily solved without calling in a professional. In your prompt, explain to ChatGPT the issue you are facing and ask for details on troubleshooting or fixing. As you work on the solution, you can continue to use AI to guide you. You can even leverage its "Vision" feature by snapping a photo of your progress as you go and asking questions about what you are looking at and how to navigate it.

My toilet will not stop running after I flush it. Could you help me diagnose what the issue is and guide me through how I might get it back in working order?

IDENTIFY AND REMOVE STAINS

Ever dealt with a mysterious stain that just won't seem to come out? Or perhaps a guest accidentally spilled red wine over some white furniture. Don't panic! AI can help you not only identify the offending stain but also provide suggestions for how to effectively get rid of it. (Of course, if you already know the source of the stain and the fabric type, you can skip the addition of an image and get right into asking how to get rid of the stain.) It is also helpful to include in your prompt what the stain is on—clothing, furniture, carpet, or something else? ChatGPT will adjust its advice to the situation.

<Attach your image.> I need your help identifying this stain on my shirt, as well as the fabric that it is on. Then give me detailed guidance on how I can go about effectively removing the stain.

UNDERSTAND LAUNDRY SYMBOLS

There are over forty different "laundry symbols" that can be found on clothing tags, and they are guidelines for how to ensure the longevity of your clothing items. But what do they all mean? And with so many possible combinations, how can you know exactly the best care practice for that new item you purchased without wasting precious time searching for each symbol on Google? Just take a picture of the tag and upload it to an AI with vision capabilities using the following prompt, and you'll get your answer in no time. (P.S.: If you like to avoid complex laundry duties, this can also be helpful when you're out shopping to avoid buying any high-maintenance items.)

> <Upload your image.> What do these symbols mean for how I should care for this clothing item?

CHAPTER 4

Food, Health, and Wellness

We all know that taking care of our mental and physical health is important, yet for many of us, doing so falls low on our list of priorities, thanks to our busy lives. The time commitment associated with not only taking part in healthier actions but also *preparing* for those healthier activities can feel burdensome. Staying consistently motivated can present a challenge too. And on top of all that, if you don't know very much about topics like nutrition or fitness, your actions could be less effective and your progress might be slowed.

With the help of AI tools like ChatGPT, you can rapidly close those knowledge gaps, get inspired to take control of your health, and cut down on several tedious or time-consuming tasks. AI can also identify and begin to unblock the mental patterns or stressors that may be holding you back, and can even help you make more informed decisions about your healthcare. Of course, AI should not replace the advice of trained medical professionals.

In this chapter, you'll learn how to use ChatGPT to live a happier and healthier life. With prompt topics ranging from food shopping to healthy eating and from gamified fitness routines to getting the most out of your doctor appointments, you'll be able to make taking care of your health and well-being faster and easier.

ORGANIZE YOUR WEEKLY MEAL PLANNING AND PREP

How AI Can Help You Plan and Prep Your Meals

You probably already know that meal planning and meal prepping are fantastic ways to cut down on the total time you spend in the kitchen every week. But the "planning" part of meal prep can still be pretty time-consuming and can take a lot of mental energy! With generative AI, you can lessen the mental load by having ChatGPT develop a personalized weekly meal plan (and more!) in a matter of minutes.

Set Up Your Initial Request

Start with a simple request, detailing the number of days for which you'd like a meal plan made and what meals should be covered. You can also ask it to adjust for any dietary preferences (should meals be vegetarian? Soy-free? Kid-friendly?), allergies or food dislikes, and even how much time you have available to cook these meals. Go ahead and specify any specialty appliances you'd like to use (like an Instant Pot® or immersion blender) and the number of meals for which you'd like to use them. You can also add details for how often you'd like to repeat meals in the weekly plan to result in less prep for you!

Sample Starter Prompt

Create a 7-day vegetarian meal plan including breakfast, lunch, and dinner. Ensure that breakfast recipes take no longer than 10 minutes to make, and lunch and dinner dishes no more than 30 minutes. Meals should be repeated, but no more than 3 times during the week—for example, I am fine with having a leftover dinner for lunch. Please include at least 1 dinner that can be made with an Instant Pot®.

Get Recipes and Nutritional Breakdowns for Your Meal Plan

You will likely find your meal prep prompt results in a descriptive outline. While you could include the request for all recipes and nutritional information in your original prompt, breaking these more complicated prompts out into several prompts can often yield better results. So, in your next prompt, follow up with a request for recipes and nutritional information for items in your plan, like in the following prompt.

When asking for the recipe portions, think about not only how many people you might be prepping these meals for but also how many extra servings you might want on hand for leftovers (especially if the item is something you foresee could be batch-prepared in advance!).

If you request nutritional information in your prompt or a certain portion size, keep in mind that ChatGPT and other LLMs have some difficulty with exact math, so you shouldn't rely on them for the most accurate source of nutritional information if you are on a strict diet. They can, however, usually give you a general idea.

> Please provide me with detailed recipes for all meals in the meal plan above, portioned for 4 people, and include an approximate nutritional breakdown per serving.

Create a Grocery List from Your Meal Plan

ChatGPT can also make a consolidated grocery list of all ingredients from your weekly meal plan, using context from within your chat. This prompt is most successful when you have only generated a single meal plan and its recipes, without too many additional follow-up prompts and edits. If you have generated multiple versions of a meal plan, the AI may draw from earlier in the conversation to generate the list. Also, the measurements of ingredients might be slightly off, so it's best to double-check those tallies with your human brain.

> Based on the meal plan and recipes above, please make a complete grocery list for my week of meals, accounting for all ingredients I'll need and the appropriate amount or proportion.

Get Tips for Efficiently Prepping Your Ingredients

ChatGPT can also give you advice on how to efficiently prepare all your ingredients so you can easily assemble and cook your meals. This prompt will not only save you mental energy and time; it will also provide some helpful food storage tips that you might not know about.

> Can you list all of the ingredients for the week, sorted by recipe, that I could chop/prep in advance and store without trouble in my refrigerator until the time comes to cook the full recipe? Please also include any helpful storage tips to keep my prepped ingredients fresh. Explain your thought process.

REDUCE FOOD WASTE

How AI Can Help You Waste Less Food

Did you know according to the Recycle Track Systems company, Americans throw out approximately 120 billion pounds of food waste every year? That's about 325 pounds of waste per person annually. Luckily, AI can help you cut back on food waste to help the planet and your wallet. If you are interested in reducing your household food waste and decreasing your trips to the store, ChatGPT can provide you with helpful tips on preparing, storing, and preserving all kinds of foods to maintain their freshness as long as possible.

Set Up Your Initial Request

Whether you have an abundance of berries from a recent trip to a berry farm or a wealth of leftovers from a recent event, you can turn to ChatGPT for tips on how to keep that food item fresh. Simply tell ChatGPT what you are hoping to store or preserve, detail its current state, and ask for recommendations and tips on proper storage to increase the longevity, freshness, and safety of your food. Want a preview of some incredible tips? Try this prompt for a robust guide to food storage for common refrigerator and pantry items.

Sample Starter Prompt

Create a robust guide with tips and tricks for storing up to 20 foods commonly found in a refrigerator or pantry. For foods that can exist in multiple forms (like fresh/raw, fresh and sliced, cooked, and opened) detail tips for each stage. The goal is to teach me how to store my food in my refrigerator, pantry, or freezer to ultimately reduce food waste and trips to the store. Include little-known tips as well as any common misconceptions.

Additional Ways to Personalize

Interpret Food Labels and Food Longevity

One way to reduce food waste is to better understand the "use by" dates on food packaging. ChatGPT can help you quickly interpret food labels on different products and understand useability beyond "best by" dates, so you avoid throwing out perfectly safe food items or running to the store to replace something you already have on hand. Before you throw something out because of a food label, first consider consulting ChatGPT. You may save yourself a trip to the grocery store based on your findings!

I've got a bag of unopened quinoa that says it has a "best by" date of 3 months ago. Should I throw it out, or is it still safe to cook and consume? Is there anything I should look for to guarantee its freshness or safety? When is the last point in time it would be safe to consider consuming?

Get Recipe Ideas Using On-Hand Ingredients

Does this situation sound familiar? You've got a variety of food items in the fridge and pantry, but after a long day, figuring out how to make a meal with these seemingly random ingredients seems impossible. So you resort to another night of plain spaghetti or give in to the convenience of ordering delivery. Meanwhile, those ingredients you bought with nothing but good intentions are going bad.

Instead of falling into this trap again, ChatGPT can help you get creative in the kitchen using the items you already have on hand. Simply take an audit of your ingredients, and ChatGPT will come up with a variety of recipes you can create at home. Voice-to-text tools can be especially helpful for this prompt.

> Recommend 5 dinner recipes I could make at home using any combination of the ingredients listed below. You may assume I have common seasonings and oils on hand, as well as all common kitchen tools. I would like the recipe to not take more than an hour. These are the ingredients I have on hand— only include these items in your recommended recipes: <list the ingredients you have available>.

Learn to Use Food Scraps Effectively

A big contribution to food waste is the scraps we throw out after preparing a meal. To further reduce food waste, ChatGPT can provide you with guidance on reinventing food scraps, stale products, leftovers, and more to cut back on waste and even unlock new opportunities around the kitchen, garden, and home. Use this prompt to get inspired in a general way or just ask ChatGPT for specific in-the-moment suggestions on what you might do with an item you are considering throwing out.

> I want to cut back on food waste. Create a guide to 10 commonly wasted or thrown-out food items and provide me with inventive and effective ways to use them instead of throwing them in the trash. These can include but should not be limited to recipes.

IMPROVE YOUR COOKING

How AI Can Help You Become a Better Cook

Do you ever get tired of using the same old cooking methods you've always relied upon? Or do you find your kitchen appliances collecting dust because you just aren't sure what to do with them? Whether you are a home cook looking to expand your repertoire or a food enthusiast hoping to bring the excitement of a restaurant dining experience into your home, AI can open a door to a world of new cooking techniques and ways to accomplish them.

Set Up Your Initial Request

ChatGPT can instantly provide you with detailed guidance on how to cook your kitchen staples in new and inventive ways. Simply detail the ingredient or ingredients you are hoping to learn new cooking methods for, and/or the type of meal you are hoping to use these new techniques for, and let ChatGPT guide you to a whole new culinary experience. By including extra context on what you already know how to do, you'll avoid recommendations for cooking techniques that you're already familiar with. Notice that we're using the technique of assigning AI a specific role here (explained in Chapter 2).

Sample Starter Prompt

You are an expert chef. I'm hoping to expand my cooking repertoire at home, specifically for breakfast dishes. When making eggs, I usually only hard-boil or scramble them. Give me 10 new and inventive cooking methods for preparing eggs for breakfast. Feel free to incorporate the use of any appliances or tools that I might use in this process. For each method, give me a step-by-step guide on how to accomplish this technique.

Learn Professional Cooking Tips and Tricks

Over the years, professional and home chefs alike have discovered countless tricks around the kitchen to save time and prepare better food. AI tools, having been trained on hundreds of billions of sources, formal and user-generated alike, can access tips and tricks like these. Start with a request for 20 tips, keeping in mind you can always ask for more or expand on "why and how" for any tip in subsequent prompts.

Give me 20 little-known or obscure kitchen hacks and tips used by professional chefs that can be used by home cooks as well to prepare better food, more efficiently prepare meals, or anything else!

Learn Creative Ways to Eat More Greens

If you are trying to increase your intake of a particular type of food (say, leafy greens), this prompt can help you get over the hurdle of becoming bored with your consumption or resistant to adopting new foods that you traditionally have not enjoyed.

I am trying to incorporate more leafy greens into my diet, but I have quite an aversion to them after a childhood of plain steamed vegetables. Give me 10 inventive ways to easily incorporate leafy greens into my diet so that I don't taste them or so that they actually taste good! Please outline the method for each approach.

Scale Recipes Up and/or Down with Cooking Conversions

If you need to convert your recipe into a larger or smaller portion, AI can help! Just input the amounts of each ingredient into ChatGPT, then note the serving size of the recipe and the desired serving size you would like to make. Note: While major LLMs are getting more reliable with math-related questions, they can still hallucinate. Adding "explain your thought process" gives these tools a little extra permission to take time when logically processing the request.

ChatGPT Plus is currently best with requests like these, thanks to its data analytics feature. Claude AI is also pretty consistently reliable as well.

> The ingredients provided serve 6, but I would like to make a serving for just 2 people. Please convert all the ingredients to the proper size to reflect this change in portion. Explain your thought process for each conversion.

Understand How to Use Your Kitchen Appliances

Many of us have a kitchen appliance or two collecting dust on a shelf because we don't know what to do with it. The prospect of understanding the ins and outs of various settings on the appliance can feel a bit overwhelming—or maybe we've simply lost the instruction manual! With a prompt to ChatGPT, you can unlock a massive amount of instant inspiration for easy recipes the appliance is best at, and even unpack when to use each of the settings.

> A year ago, I bought an Instant Pot® Duo Crisp 11-in-1 Air Fryer, but I've barely used it. All of the settings and buttons intimidate me. Could you make a guide to the 11 settings and what each one does? Then provide me with 10 recipes (with detailed instructions) that I can try using the different methods.

Discover New Ways to Use Common Kitchen Appliances

If you're looking for ways to get more out of your kitchen appliances, ChatGPT can share countless little-known kitchen hacks for using them. You can start by requesting a general guide to little-known tips for common kitchen appliances and tools or go more in-depth with specific requests for certain appliances' capabilities, like your blender or slow cooker.

> You are an expert professional chef known for your extensive knowledge of surprising ways to use kitchen appliances and make the cooking process more efficient and inventive. Share with me 20 little-known tips and hacks for how I can use any of the following appliances: rice cooker, broiler, coffee maker, blender, slow cooker.

CREATE A FITNESS PLAN

How AI Can Help You Create a Fitness Plan

When you are ready to start a new fitness routine, ChatGPT can be a knowledgeable, nonjudgmental resource for both basic and more advanced information. Whether you want a long-term training schedule, exercise suggestions, or motivation, you can find guidance set up just for you.

Set Up Your Initial Request

Start with a clear summary of where you are and what you would like your goal to be. Having trouble getting specific? Ask ChatGPT for help in coming up with personal training ideas that might inspire you. If there are any time constraints around your goals, make those clear to ChatGPT as well. Finally, in your prompt, it is important to be honest about any limitations or restrictions you may have—do you prefer home workouts? What has motivated or demotivated you in the past during your fitness journey?

Sample Starter Prompt

You are a personal trainer specializing in fitness plans that build muscle mass in men. I am a 25-year-old man with limited strength training experience and a lean/lanky build, naturally skinny. I am ready to commit to up to 45 minutes a week of strength training, but I know I'll need to start with shorter and less frequent sessions and build up to that, based on how I'd done with new fitness plans in the past. Could you help me outline a detailed, progressive strength training plan that starts with the fundamentals and evolves over time? Please include an overview of exercises that will be most helpful to my goals.

Understand Proper Form for Exercises

After ChatGPT has produced a workout plan for you, it may have listed some exercises you've never done before. (Even if you are using a workout guide you've found elsewhere online, in your favorite health magazine, or from a friend, it is not always obvious what "proper form" means when practicing the exercise.) ChatGPT can provide incredibly detailed guidelines for the proper form and tips for getting the most out of your exercises. Beyond a written description, ChatGPT's vision feature can even provide personalized form-correction suggestions when you upload an image of yourself mid-exercise in front of a neutral background wearing more form-fitting clothes. Just tell it what exercise you are performing and say, "Please provide feedback on how to improve my <exercise> form shown in this picture."

> My workout routine includes a deadlift, and while I understand the basic idea, I want to be sure I have the best possible form when approaching this exercise. Please explain what the proper form for a deadlift is, as well as any tips for doing this exercise effectively. I'd also like your help in understanding how I can determine which weight amount and rep count may be most effective for me for this exercise.

Craft Nutrition Plans That Align with Your Fitness Goals

Fitness goals and your nutritional intake go hand in hand. Whether you're running a marathon, boosting your muscle mass, or losing weight, AI can help you determine what to eat to support your training plans. While ChatGPT cannot replace a professional human nutritionist, it can explain the basics of what you should consider to fuel specific fitness goals. You can also ask it to generate meal plans and guidelines suited to those goals. It can also offer fun new recipe ideas to keep you motivated if you're pursuing a change in diet. Keep in mind that AI's mathematical predictions (like calorie counts) are estimates at best. Plan to pair your nutritional inspiration from AI with other nutrition tracking and food measurement tools.

I am a 5-foot-6-inch, 140-pound woman training for a marathon. My routine includes 40 miles of running and 3 hours of cross-training weekly. I aim to maintain or slightly increase muscle while focusing on endurance and recovery. Please provide a detailed nutrition plan, emphasizing macronutrient balance for marathon training, along with a week's sample meal plan tailored to my training needs and goals.

Create a Post-Workout Recovery Guide

Proper recovery-focused nutrition, stretches, and time are essential when practicing a fitness routine. From suggesting the right balance of nutrients to aid muscle repair and growth to recommending stretches that target the muscles you've just worked the hardest, ChatGPT can help ensure your recovery is effective and comprehensive so that you can avoid overtraining and injuries. Beyond your regular fitness routine, basic stretching is important for general flexibility and stress release. Spend all day sitting at your desk? ChatGPT can suggest stretches to help with posture and muscle tension built up from stress.

In about a week, I will be going snow skiing for the first time (starting with some beginner skiing lessons). While I stay relatively fit with home workouts and walking, I expect learning this new skill to be physically grueling. Please create a post-skiing recovery guide, including recommended stretches or other recovery techniques, to ensure I can return to the slopes every day of my 4-day trip.

PROVIDE EMOTIONAL SUPPORT AND GUIDANCE

How AI Can Help You Deal with Stressful Periods

If you are dealing with increased stress in your daily life, AI tools like ChatGPT can prove to be an excellent resource. While ChatGPT lacks the "life context" that friends, partners, and therapists have, it can also offer an on-demand "listening ear" and act as an objective sounding board for your stressors.

Similarly, you can be honest with what you input into ChatGPT, without fearing judgment or retribution for what you say in a moment of stress. Much like journaling, simply writing or speaking out your feelings into the world can be a great way to manage your feelings, and ChatGPT offers the experience of responding while also being objective.

Set Up Your Initial Request

For this use case, I find it particularly helpful to leverage the voice-to-text functionality of ChatGPT. Simply turn that on and begin to talk. You don't have to follow any formal structure when prompting ChatGPT like this—just speak as if you were sharing with a trusted friend. You need not even make a request of ChatGPT after you "let it all out" if you don't want to. I've found that when you "say" something to ChatGPT without asking it for anything, it will respond as a sympathetic ear and maybe even offer advice anyway.

Sample Starter Prompt

<Describe your situation in however much detail you like! Just let it out—it doesn't have to be well structured. Then add a request like:>
  Could you provide me with some advice on how to handle this situation?
  I just need you to play the role of a best friend and hype me up and say I'm totally right because honestly I'm really frustrated and just need to vent. Only provide very subtle advice. Can you do that?

I need to get out of my head—can you talk to me in a way that will help me calm down? Please keep your answers somewhat short and give me something to respond to as we talk.

Could you provide me with a strategy for overcoming this problem over the next month?

Additional Ways to Personalize

Suggest Thought-Provoking Questions

Cognitive-behavioral is a type of "talk therapy" that is particularly effective at helping to manage symptoms of some mental health conditions (such as anxiety disorders) by reframing negative thoughts. While AI tools are not as effective as a human therapist who can follow you over time and spot nuances throughout your interactions to inform your growth, ChatGPT can help you brainstorm ideas while you wait to talk to a professional. When leveraging this prompt, you'll not only be asking ChatGPT to play a role; you'll also be training it on how best to respond to you, mostly by taking the reins of the conversation and guiding it to focus solely on asking thoughtful follow-up questions and helping drive you to your own conclusions and solutions through that dialogue.

I need you to play the role of a cognitive-behavioral therapist. I've been struggling with <describe your situation>. Could you help me by asking insightful questions that lead me to understand my thought patterns and behaviors around this issue, while helping to guide me to solutions? Please keep your responses concise, focusing on asking great questions to uncover deeper nuances in my situation, rather than providing lengthy advice or solutions. Ask me 1–2 questions per response, and occasionally offer advice.

Offer Alternative Perspectives and Mindset Reframing

We can all sometimes see things through tunnel vision. When you're in periods of heightened stress or emotion, it can be difficult to take a step back and see things a little differently. AI can help you do just that, so you can feel more at ease, improve your relationships with others, live more in the present, and shift your focus to what is *really* most important. ChatGPT can also instantly provide you with different takes on situations that can aid in the process of healing or calming down. In your first prompt, using voice-to-text or typing directly, provide as much detail as you are comfortable with about the situation. Then append your previous prompt with any of the following examples.

Even though I'm really mad at this person, I do care about them and want to believe they didn't do this to hurt me. Could you provide me with some alternative perspectives and explanations for their behavior?

For all of these reasons, I feel like my boss is out to get me, even if that seems illogical. What are some other explanations for her actions that I may not be seeing?

I feel like I'll never reach my goals, and nothing has been going right lately even though I'm sure logically *something* is. Can you help me find things that are going right in my life by asking me a few questions at a time, like a conversation, to help me reframe my focus on the good?

Create Personalized Positive Affirmations

Positive affirmations that you can write down or repeat to yourself can be a powerful way to stay focused on the good things around you. With a simple prompt, ChatGPT can generate a series of phrases customized to your specific situation. And you can get ChatGPT to craft these phrases in whatever format most appeals to you—a rhyming couplet? A longer motivational mantra? Punchy, short, and sweet? Maybe a little sassy? The possibilities are unlimited.

I am trying to reframe my mindset to feel more confident at work. Please come up with 10 rhyming positive affirmations for me to choose from.

I want to feel more confident in my own skin. Please come up with 10 mantras that I can say in the morning to help me remember my beauty, inside and out.

I need 10 quippy and short phrases to motivate me both in my workouts and at my job when faced with a challenge. I want to shift my mindset to "I can do hard things" or to believe hard things are easy.

PREPARE FOR A MEDICAL VISIT

How AI Can Help You Prepare for a Medical Visit

Whether it's a standard checkup with your primary care physician or a visit to a specialist, doctors' appointments can be stressful and overwhelming. Even a visit to the medical building or hospital can feel nerve-racking. AI can help you both before the appointment (to organize your thoughts, record any symptoms or specific situations, and brainstorm questions to ask) and after it (to fully understand what you were told and learn how to follow up if necessary).

Set Up Your Initial Request

Start by telling AI about the upcoming visit. Who are you seeing and why? Outline your overall health status going into the appointment. Do you have concerns you want to be sure to address? Do you need help addressing any feelings of nervousness, shyness, or even panic?

Sample Starter Prompt

I have an appointment next week with my primary care physician. I want to ask them about the headaches I have been getting more frequently. I always get so nervous at the doctor's office, though, and find myself either not saying how I really feel or downplaying my symptoms. How can I approach it with more confidence?

Additional Ways to Personalize

Generate a List of Questions to Ask Your Doctor

Have you ever left a doctor's appointment and thought, "Oh, shoot! I should have asked about that one thing!" Whether you have a medical procedure coming up or you are just getting a regular check-up and have some outstanding health questions, ChatGPT can help by providing you with a robust list of questions to ask your doctor so that you can get the most out of your visit and leave feeling confident about your medical decisions and next steps. Whether you use these prompts the night before or in the waiting room, ChatGPT can help you leave no question unanswered.

> I'm considering getting elective dental crowns for my front teeth and want to ensure I cover all bases during my next dental appointment. Could you help me compile a list of important questions to ask my dentist about the procedure, such as expected outcomes, side effects, maintenance, potential risks, how it might affect my overall oral health, and expected costs in the near term and long term?

Understand What to Expect Before and After a Medical Procedure

If you have a medical procedure coming up that you are worried about, knowing what to expect can be a great way to ease your anxiety. ChatGPT can not only help guide you through the procedure itself; it can also provide helpful tips on how to prepare for it and what a typical recovery looks like.

> I'm scheduled for a procedure that requires general anesthesia, and it's my first time undergoing any form of sedation. I'm uneasy about the anesthesia itself—how it feels to be under it, the potential side effects, and how I'll feel afterward. Could you explain the process of receiving anesthesia, what I can expect during the induction and awakening phases, and tips for recovery post-anesthesia?

Understand Medical Terms

Have you ever seen blood test results with confusing numbers and lingo? Or heard a medical term thrown around in passing by your doctor or included on your medical chart? Most of us don't understand the countless medical terms and jargon we're exposed to, and we are left wondering, "Huh? What does *that* mean?" With a simple query to prompt ChatGPT, you can find out what these terms mean quickly and easily and ask follow-up questions about what you've learned.

My blood test results say my LDL cholesterol is marked as 140 mg/dL. Can you explain what LDL cholesterol is and what it means for it to be at this level? Also, what are the normal ranges, and what steps can I take if it's considered high?

CREATE NEW AND INVENTIVE DISHES

If you like to experiment in the kitchen, ChatGPT can act as your partner in crime. In your prompt, include details on the type of dish you are interested in creating (breakfast, dessert, appetizer, cocktail, etc.) and list the ingredients you have on hand, including those that you think might be a nontraditional but interesting addition to your recipe.

> Acting as a *MasterChef* contestant, I would like your assistance in creating 3 potential inventive (but delicious) unconventional dessert recipes. I have all of the common ingredients for baking in my pantry, but I also have the following less typical ingredients: Oreos, loose-leaf tea (oolong, Earl Grey, and lavender), apples, raspberries, Brie, rum, and whiskey. In each recipe, include up to two of my less typical ingredients.

CREATE AN ORGANIZED GROCERY LIST

Every week, I make my grocery lists in just a few minutes, with as little manual or mental effort as possible, using ChatGPT. When I'm ready to head to the store, I tap the "microphone" button in my app so that I can perform a verbal audit of everything I need from the store. When combined with this prompt, ChatGPT will not only summarize my ramblings into a clear list; it will also sort all the items into the appropriate grocery aisle. Now I waste no time doubling back to get produce I forget when I'm already in the frozen section!

> I am about to look through my fridge and pantry and rattle off all the things I need to purchase at the grocery store. I need you to create a grocery list of everything I need to buy, sorted by the aisle or section in which these items would appear.

SUGGEST HEALTHIER WAYS TO COOK YOUR FAVORITE MEALS

If you are trying to eat healthier, ChatGPT can suggest healthier methods to prepare your favorite foods and even generate better-for-you recipes for your favorite "comfort food" classics with ingredient swaps that taste almost as good as the real thing. You can also try this for seasonal recipes or special-event food, like appetizers for the Super Bowl.

I am focusing on trying to eat healthier, but I miss my favorite comfort foods—fried chicken and mac and cheese. Could you provide me with 3 alternative ways and recipes to prepare each of these dishes in a way that is a little healthier, and explain what makes each method healthier than the traditional prep? I'd like each of the recipes to taste and feel as close to the "real thing" as possible.

FIND INGREDIENT SUBSTITUTIONS

When you're in the middle of a recipe and realize that you've run out of an ingredient you need, AI can save the day. Tell it what you're making, the ingredient you're out of, and ask it to supply some alternatives that might work for your situation.

I am trying to make a cake but just realized I need 2 eggs and I'm all out of them. What ingredients can I use instead that will work in a cake?

CRAFT A CUSTOM WORKOUT PLAYLIST FOR DIFFERENT EXERCISES

Nothing motivates a workout like a great playlist! While music-streaming platforms offer countless public playlists to search from, there's also something special about making your own. With the help of AI, you can create a playlist customized to your music taste, motivations, and workout pace. In crafting your prompt, include details on the genres of songs you like, any artists you are particularly fond of, the general pace of your workout (do you want music that's energizing for jogging or calming for yoga?), and details on themes or emotions you'd like to incorporate. You should also mention if there are any genres or artists you'd like to avoid.

Can you create a playlist of 30 motivating songs for strength training at the gym? The tracks should have lyrics about "not caring what others think" to help me stay focused and empowered. The songs should have a good rhythm suitable for strength exercises, with a strong beat and pace but not overly long. I prefer music that keeps me pumped and determined throughout my workout. I do not like country music.

VARY YOUR FITNESS ROUTINE WITH A RANDOM EXERCISE GENERATOR

Have you ever seen those card decks or dice designed to add a touch of random variety to your workout routine? They consist of exercises and rep counts for you to perform based on what you randomly draw or roll, and they can mix up your routine and make it more fun. ChatGPT offers this same service, giving you random exercises to complete, either one at a time or in a sequence. You can also easily customize your random workout generator to your workout preferences and available equipment.

> Let's play a game. You are a random workout generator. Each time I tell you "Go!" you will assign me a random exercise task to complete as well as details on reps or the amount of time to spend doing the exercise. Each task should be estimated to take about 30 seconds to 2 minutes to complete. Tasks could be bodyweight exercises, exercises requiring free weights, or treadmill exercises. I am moderately fit and like a challenge. Ready? Go!

UNDERSTAND AND SOOTHE COMMON SYMPTOMS

Have you ever suddenly felt "off" in some way? Maybe you don't quite feel sick to the point that you'd necessarily head to the doctor, but still, something is making you feel like you aren't at your 100% peak health. While it's certainly not a replacement for a real doctor, ChatGPT can be helpful in situations like this. Start by telling AI about the symptoms you're experiencing—describe them as best you can, discuss how long you've had them, and detail their severity. Ask the tool to follow up with questions you can answer to give it more specific details. Once you've determined what the problem might be, you can ask AI for at-home solutions or even natural remedies.

> This morning I woke up with the slightest tickle in my throat, and one of my nostrils felt a little stuffy, but also itchy. The other strange thing is when I flare my nostril, it hurts a little bit and is sore when I touch it from the outside. What could be going on? Am I getting the flu or could it be something else? Please unpack what I could be experiencing and ask follow-up questions to help you explore some possible explanations.

TACKLE MENTAL OVERWHELM WITH A TO-DO LIST

There's always so much to do and so little time to do it! When you are feeling so overwhelmed by all of the things on your plate that you don't even have time to make an actual to-do list, ChatGPT can help you tackle swirling thoughts and sort and organize your tasks into a list that's manageable and actionable. Start with the following prompt accompanied by a "mind dump" of all the tasks that have piled up. I highly recommend the voice-to-text feature for this! ChatGPT will listen and consolidate your brain dump into a nicely organized and prioritized list. Once you've got your sorted and prioritized list from ChatGPT, you can take this list a step further by asking it to create an actionable, time-specific schedule to accomplish everything on your list.

> I've got so much on my plate! I'm going to ramble for a bit and list out everything that is stressing me out that I have to get done at some point. I need you to help me sort and prioritize all of these tasks based on what seems to be the most important task based on the context I provide. <List out everything you can think of with as much context as possible, including if any hot deadlines are driving extra urgency.> Please also provide tips on breaking these loftier and bigger tasks into smaller, more manageable tasks.

CHAPTER 5

Career Development and the Workplace

According to some estimates, the average person spends about 90,000 hours of their life at work. That's a huge slice of your lifetime's pie! You may be aware that AI tools can boost your productivity during those working hours, freeing up your brain for bigger thinking instead of performing tedious tasks—but did you know generative AI can also bolster your career growth?

In this chapter, we'll cover a myriad of ways AI tools can help you position yourself for the jobs that interest you, interview and negotiate like a pro, and progress in your career by refining your work communications, getting guidance on career development, and expanding your professional network.

When you enlist AI's help in your career journey, you'll learn to navigate the nuances of the workplace and career ladder with knowledgeable guidance, no matter your industry or role. With the help of AI, you'll think bigger, communicate better, and discover opportunities you may not have considered before. With the prompts in this chapter, you'll have the tools you need to leverage AI to guide you on a path that will make those 90,000 hours worth all that effort.

APPLY FOR JOBS

How AI Can Help You with the Job Application Process

Applying for jobs can be a grueling process, especially if you don't have an "in" at the company. Applying quickly with a resume that reflects that you are a match for the job's description can greatly help your chances of getting an interview—especially considering that many companies use AI to read and sort resumes. Put AI to work for *you* and craft strong and keyword-filled resumes, faster than ever!

Set Up Your Initial Request

The two core elements of a successful prompt for this topic are (1) your current resume and (2) the job description you are applying for. If you are using a tool that allows for direct attachments in your chat, you can simply attach your resume and/or job description and reference them in your prompt. If you cannot provide attachments, copying and pasting the content directly into the chat will usually work just as well.

Sample Starter Prompt

You are an expert in crafting resumes for senior software engineer roles in lean tech startups. I need your assistance in rewriting my resume with strong action verbs that align with the job description of the role for which I'm applying.

Keep all bullets concise and results-driven—no more than 2 lines, but ideally 1 line each. Do not remove any part of the resume; merely conduct rewrites. Please also incorporate important keywords and phrases from the job description into my resume and rewrite where you can to help optimize my resume for the role.

My current resume is here: "<copy + paste, or attach>."

And the job description is here: "<copy + paste, or attach>."

Spot Opportunities to Improve Your Resume

If you don't have an up-to-date resume to work with, or your existing resume is strong but not well suited for this particular role, you can follow up this first prompt with another to engage ChatGPT as a collaborative partner in making your resume even stronger for this job application.

What keywords from the job description above are not currently captured in the resume? First, suggest how I might authentically incorporate these keywords. Second, please ask me any questions about my work experience that would, once answered, help me come up with stronger bullet points to match this job description.

Draft Customized Cover Letters

A personalized and well-written cover letter can go a long way in making a strong impression on a potential employer or a company recruiter. However, if you are in the middle of a job application process, the time it takes to craft a cover letter could slow your progress. ChatGPT can help you produce personalized cover letters faster, giving you a great framework and structure to edit and submit or just to provide inspiration for overcoming writer's block.

I need your assistance crafting a concise and thoughtful cover letter that speaks to my qualifications for the role to which I am applying, my enthusiasm for the role, and what I will uniquely bring to it. It should not exceed 3 paragraphs. The tone should be professional, confident, and enthusiastic. The opening of the letter should hook the reader, and the letter should maintain their interest throughout. My current resume and the job description are attached/pasted below. More details about myself that make me a good fit for the role include <type or speak your qualifications>.

Receive Feedback on Your Cover Letter

Want to take it a step further? Using the cover letter you've written or edited, whether with ChatGPT or on your own, you can seek feedback from ChatGPT on the letter and how you might improve on it before sending it off. This prompt can also be used for feedback on your resume, a follow-up email to the hiring team, and more!

> I need feedback on my cover letter. Acting as a professional career coach, please provide me with thoughtful and detailed feedback on changes I should make to improve this cover letter and hopefully secure an interview for this role. Also detail if there are any errors or consideration terms of structure, spelling, grammar, and so on that I should adjust. The cover letter is here: <paste or attach>. And the job description is here: <paste or attach>.

PRACTICE INTERVIEWING

How AI Can Help You Interview Confidently

Whether it has been a while since you last interviewed, or you just want to polish your interview skills and be prepared for anything thrown at you, ChatGPT can help you prepare.

Set Up Your Initial Request

If you provide ChatGPT with the details of the job description and your interviewer, ChatGPT can generate a list of interview questions with which you can practice. Once you have your list of questions, you can begin to think about how you might answer them in preparation for your upcoming interview.

I have a 30-minute informational interview with an internal recruiter for a product manager role. The job description for this role is attached and pasted below. I need you to make a list of 10 potential questions I might be asked by this recruiter at this early stage in the process. Please also provide me with 10 questions I should consider asking the recruiter, as well as any advice you may have on navigating this first call when it comes to compensation, role expectations, and my qualifications.

Additional Ways to Personalize

Simulate a Practice Interview

Job interviews can be very nerve-racking. In just about 30 minutes, you have to simultaneously make an impression beyond your resume and convince the interviewer that you are qualified for the role and a good fit for the company culture. Interviewing is (without a doubt) a skill, and it can always be developed. Believe it or not, ChatGPT can help you develop those skills by conducting a simulated interview with you and giving you feedback on your responses! Start with the following prompt to prime the chat, then use the voice-to-text functionality of your AI tool to practice actually speaking your answers out loud.

I would like you to conduct a simulated practice interview with me for an account manager position. I will be interviewing with the director of sales. For this simulated interview, you should act as the director of sales, asking me questions this person would be likely to ask me. Only ask one question at a time, then wait for my response.

Once my response is in, please structure your next response as:

Feedback: (Here you will provide me with advice on what was good about the answer and what might have made it better, from the interviewer's perspective.)

Next question: (Here you will ask another question from the director of sale's point of view.)

We'll continue in this way until I am ready to end the simulated interview. I have <attached/pasted> the job description for reference.

Get More In-Depth Feedback and Suggested Adjustments

If you would like to dive deeper into any of the feedback provided to you, you can always pause your interview simulation to ask further follow-up questions and seek more advice. Once you've got your answers, you can pick back up where the "interview" left off by asking ChatGPT to jump back into the role it was previously playing and continue the simulation with a new question.

Let's pause this interview for a moment. I will tell you when we can continue this simulation. While we are paused, I would like you to provide me with more coaching on my last answer—what are 3 alternative ways I could have better structured that response?

NEGOTIATE HIGHER COMPENSATION

How AI Can Help You Increase Your Salary

Whether you are on the job hunt for a horizontal move or vertical jump—or simply looking to understand what you might be able to earn in a similar role somewhere else—getting a good idea of the market rate for someone in your role or at your current level of experience is very important. AI can help you determine your market rate and make a case for an increase in compensation as you evaluate new roles or have career conversations.

Set Up Your Initial Request

In your first prompt, provide details on your title, industry, years of experience, education level, and any special skills or experience you have to offer that are rare in your field. If you leverage an AI with web-browsing capabilities, you can get a rough idea of the going rate for your skills on the market and receive suggestions on where to go to dig in deeper.

Sample Starter Prompt

I am a social media manager based in Austin, Texas, with 5 years of experience developing content and social media strategy for online CPG (consumer packaged goods) brands on Instagram and TikTok, with a total following of about 60,000 followers at my current company. I have a bachelor's degree in communications from UT Austin. Help me estimate the current standard market-rate salary range for someone like me. Explain your thought process and then suggest how I can find up-to-date estimates online to back up this estimate.

Additional Ways to Personalize

Compare Two Offers

Being offered a role at a new company is very exciting, but before you accept the role, it is important to fully understand your offer and its value. You probably also want to compare it to the benefits packages at your current role or other roles you are considering. With the help of AI, you can get a measured take on the overall strength of your offer and unpack considerations for your particular situation. In your prompt, give as much detail as you possibly can on the two opportunities you are comparing, including base salary, bonus structure, healthcare benefits, total coverage, paid time off, retirement matching, and more.

I am considering 2 job offers and need help evaluating which job will likely be the best option to choose in the next 5 years, both from a financial standpoint and a career growth standpoint. Here are the details for Job 1: <provide details on salary, bonus, healthcare benefits, PTO policy, stock options, etc.>. And here are the details for Job 2: <provide details>.

Evaluate Total Compensation

Please provide an analysis of the financial and nonfinancial pros and cons of each option, as well as any other considerations I may be missing. Additionally, calculate the approximate annual value of both compensation packages and explain your thought process. Finally, ask me further questions if needed to help you make this comparison.

Negotiate a Job Offer

According to a 2022 survey by Fidelity, approximately 85% of Americans who negotiated their offer received at least some of what they were asking for. However, a 2023 report from Glassdoor revealed a full 54% of American professionals accepted their more recent role without negotiating. Lack of confidence in your negotiating skills or a discomfort with the negotiation process can have a major impact on your current and future earnings. You can overcome whatever is holding you back by asking ChatGPT for guidance, such as helping with evaluating offers, advising you through the negotiation process, and drafting negotiation emails or speaking points. Use the following prompt as a starting point, and then follow up with additional questions to get specific advice on prioritizing what and how to negotiate for your job offer.

I just got a job offer, and I plan to accept, but I've heard negotiating can help me secure an even better offer. I don't know the first thing about negotiating, but I feel like I should try to negotiate more. Provide me with a robust guide to negotiation with sections on (1) How to approach negotiation effectively, (2) What I might ask for and how I might ask, (3) Any tips on negotiating things outside of salary, and (4) How to prepare myself mentally for this and what to expect, given I have not negotiated like this in the past.

REVIEW AND NEGOTIATE CONTRACTS

How AI Can Help with Contract Negotiation

Have you ever been in a situation at work where you needed to sign a contract but felt overwhelmed by the legal jargon and concerned about any hidden clauses? In most situations, contracts are negotiable. AI can not only help you interpret and understand the legal repercussions of a contract and its clauses; it can also help you spot items in the contract that may not benefit you and provide suggestions on how to adjust the contract to better suit your needs.

To be clear: AI is not a substitute for a professional lawyer, but if you need minor contracts negotiated, AI can help you know what to expect for your obligations in a contract, how to protect yourself, and when things are complex enough to warrant official legal counsel.

Set Up Your Initial Request

Start by uploading the uncopyrighted contents of the contract into any AI tool that can reference and read attachments, like Claude AI or ChatGPT. From there, ask for a high-level summary of key information found in the contract as well as any important obligations or conditions. Providing additional information about who you are in the context of the contract, how you interpret the agreement, and what you are most concerned about can be helpful details to add to your prompt.

Sample Starter Prompt

I am a social media content creator evaluating a contract from a potential sponsor. I have attached the contract here. I need your help providing a clear summary of my obligations for this contract, as well as the obligations of the other party and any significant conditions or penalties involved.

Uncover Potential Issues or Unfair Clauses

Before signing a contract, it is crucial to make sure your interests are represented as fairly and reasonably as possible. AI can specifically look for clauses that may be unreasonably favorable to the other party or expose you to risk and neatly summarize them for you. It can also explain potential repercussions if you kept the contract as is.

Now please detail specifically any sections or clauses that may not work in my best interest, could be considered unfair, or could expose me to significant risk. Explain why you have flagged each section (why it is not in my best interest) and what could happen if it remains as it is in the contract.

Suggest Adjustments to Negotiate in the Contract

Once you know what parts of the contract would be best for you to negotiate to better protect yourself, you can ask AI to suggest revisions for each item. You may also request that it consider where else you might add additional terms to the contract to protect your interests.

For each item you have noted, propose any changes or redlines I should request to protect myself and/or my social media brand and business when working with this company. Also let me know if anything is missing from this contract that I should ask to include in order to protect my interests.

Draft an Email Detailing the Requested Changes

Now that you know what changes need to be made in the contract, you can ask ChatGPT to draft a professional and emotion-free response detailing all changes requested for the contract and the reasoning behind each request.

Draft a cordial and professional email for me to send to the other party, detailing all the suggested changes you have recommended to me. Clearly outline them, referencing in what section they appear in the contract, and include a short justification for each reason behind this request. Include an appropriate greeting and sign-off, emphasizing my eagerness to work together and sign the contract once these adjustments are made.

DRAFT YEAR-END REVIEWS

How AI Can Help You Write Great Year-End Reviews

Your annual self-review is an opportunity for you to summarize your accomplishments and emphasize your value. You may even want to make the case for a raise or promotion. Still, so many of us struggle with both the time it takes to write a strong summary and the idea of "bragging" about ourselves. With the help of AI tools, you can conquer both tasks with relative ease.

Set Up Your Initial Request

For the best results, it's helpful to have a document that you've kept throughout the year detailing your core accomplishments and the impacts you've made. You can attach that document to your prompt in an AI tool that supports attachments (like Claude or ChatGPT). If you lack such a document, take 15 minutes to reflect on your biggest areas of influence and accomplishments since the previous review cycle. This does not have to be incredibly neat—bullet points, stream of consciousness, and so on are all fine.

From there, use this starter prompt to restructure your list of accomplishments into a strong self-review, which you should edit and adjust before submitting. This method will save time by helping you overcome writer's block to structure your first draft. It also allows you to take a bit of a step back as you get used to writing about your successes.

Attached is a document detailing my proudest accomplishments from projects in the past year at my job. I need your help writing an annual self-performance review. Read, organize, and summarize from my document what you see as the key themes for how I have improved, grown, and made a positive impact on the business in the past year. Keep in mind that this will be read by my manager and potentially their managers, so make sure that the review is both clear and digestible for someone who may lack the extreme level of detail that I have included. My goal in this review is to frame myself as a high performer deserving of a salary increase in the coming year.

Additional Ways to Personalize ──○

Answer Specific Questions for Your Review

Once you've done your initial summary, you can get help drafting answers to specific questions listed on your performance review. Ask AI to do so in whatever framework your manager prefers, from standard paragraphs to bullet points, or any other summary framework.

I will now provide you with a series of questions about my past performance. For each question I give you, draft a response using context from my uploaded document. My manager prefers simple bullet points in these answers, with a clear focus on my contributions and what impact they made. Here is the first question: <paste the first question>.

Draft 360 Reviews or Performance Reviews for Others

If your job requires that you participate in 360 reviews where you review other coworkers (both above, beside, and under you in the company hierarchy), or if you have to write performance reviews for a large team, AI can expedite this process while also guaranteeing your feedback is in the proper form and tone. You may have notes prepared that AI can use to help summarize as you did for your self-review. Alternatively, to save even more time, you can use voice-to-text functionality in your AI tool to speak aloud your questions and your honest answer to each of them about those being reviewed. AI will help you transform your dictated answer into thoughtfully written, constructive reviews.

> I need your help drafting a fair and balanced 360 review for my coworker. I am going to read off each question in my review process one at a time, then speak out loud my thoughts on the answer. It will likely be a little long-winded. After I have gone through all my questions, you can keep the "Q&A" format, but please make my answers more concise, focusing on my coworker's strengths or areas of opportunities and leveraging specific examples from my answers where relevant <Begin asking and answering the questions.>

IMPROVE PROFESSIONAL COMMUNICATIONS

How AI Can Help You Communicate Effectively in the Workplace

With the rise of tools like Slack and Microsoft Teams and the fact that more and more people are working remotely, many professionals find themselves communicating with the written word more often than in person or verbally. This situation can create a unique challenge to team building and fostering a collaborative environment with clear communication.

From conveying a professional tone in written text to providing a clear and concise summary to your teammates or leaders, ChatGPT can help you communicate effectively and efficiently, so you can spend less time mulling over how to phrase communications and more time doing your actual job.

Set Up Your Initial Request

There are myriad ways you can prompt ChatGPT to help you communicate better or reframe communications you have drafted. In your prompt, include the communication you have drafted (in quotation marks to distinguish your writing from the prompt request). Alternatively, you may simply share the gist of what you are trying to say. Then indicate the goal of your communication and in what way you'd like to be interpreted: Collaborative? Friendly but authoritative? Firm and clear? Finally, give a rough indication of the appropriate length for your response (to avoid overly wordy suggestions from ChatGPT). Then ask ChatGPT to draft a response. For short messages, you may even ask for three variations of the message so you have options to pick from and tweak to your liking before you send it off.

Sample Starter Prompt

I've been asked by my boss to take on another new project at work from a coworker who I think is slacking. While I'm glad to help, I already have too much on my plate and cannot possibly take on more work without removing something else. Please help me draft 3 distinct messages (short, professional, and concise—no more than 4 sentences) I can send my boss that set a firm tone but still sound collaborative. Suggest any additional tips for communicating around this scenario.

Additional Ways to Personalize

Analyze and Adjust Your Tone of Voice

Have you ever gotten feedback that you come off as abrasive, rude, or blunt in your messaging? ChatGPT can suggest ways to improve your language to get a better reaction from your teammates. Or maybe you worry that others perceive you as unconfident or a pushover? ChatGPT can help you catch the phrases that may contribute to that and guide you to write something stronger. By taking an extra moment to have ChatGPT analyze the tone of something you are about to send before you send it, you can tackle most communication problems before they arise.

Could you analyze the tone of the message that I've shared in the quotations below? My coworker and I disagree on a business decision, and I am trying to get them to come over to my side and see reason. Executives are on this channel, so I want to sound professional and not be perceived as negative or disrespectful to my teammate (even though I'm internally rolling my eyes). Please analyze the tone, then provide suggestions to improve the message. Here is my message: "<Paste in your message>."

Condense Your Communications for Executive Eyes

If you are trying to rise in your career, being able to communicate clearly and effectively with as few words as possible is an important skill to hone. Although you are no doubt aware of all the nitty-gritty details of a project, the executives from which you need buy-in or support, or to whom you need to provide an update, often just need the facts.

AI tools can be immensely helpful in this endeavor, especially if you struggle with boiling things down to just the basics. You can take an existing draft of your writing and throw it into ChatGPT with the following prompt.

Below I've pasted some communications I have drafted for my department's VP on a situation at work they need the details on. I need it to be shorter as a high-level executive summary, keeping only the details that are necessary for executive understanding. My goal in sharing this is <your goal>. Here is what I have so far: <paste in your writing>.

Save Time Giving Written Updates

For more in-the-moment communications, you may not already have something written down. When your boss sends you a message asking for an update (and wants it fast), it may be difficult to quickly draft a perfectly written summary. In this instance, you can pull up your favorite AI tool, dictate your update and all the details into the voice-to-text functionality, and have AI create a nice executive summary for you to send to your boss. For a little extra flair, you can request that the final synopsis be formatted in a particular summarization framework like SCQA (situation, complication, question, answer), the 5 W's and H (who, what, where, when, why, and how), STAR (situation, task, action, result) or anything else your heart (or your boss) desires.

I am going to ramble a little bit about a situation at work that I need to update my department VP on. My goal is <your goal>. I need you to consolidate my ramblings into a concise executive-level summary, keeping only what details are necessary. Here's the situation: <describe your situation>.

EVALUATE NEW OPPORTUNITIES

How AI Can Help You Explore New Career Paths

Have you been feeling stuck in your career or maybe curious about exploring a new line of work? Or perhaps you're tired of reporting to someone else and want to be your own boss? Like a great career or life coach, ChatGPT can act as both an excellent sounding board and a guiding light to help you explore and evaluate alternative career paths or entrepreneurial opportunities aligned with your passions and unique skill sets.

Set Up Your Initial Request

For your first prompt, provide ChatGPT with details on your current role; a quick summary of your skill sets and day-to-day tasks; and some context around what you find frustrating, demotivating, or draining about your current position. The more context you can provide on your current situation, goals, skills, and what you are looking for, the more helpful ChatGPT can be in guiding you. Then you can tell ChatGPT to ask you a few more questions, which will enable ChatGPT to give you more personalized coaching.

Sample Starter Prompt

You are an expert career coach. I'm looking for guidance to pivot from my current role as a social media manager at a large corporate home supplies company to a more strategic and cross-functional position, perhaps even at a different kind of company. Before we begin, please ask me 10 questions to better understand my career goals, preferences, and skill sets so that you can make recommendations for new paths to consider exploring.

Get Specific Recommendations

Once you've been asked questions by your AI career coach, answer them honestly and efficiently using the voice-to-text feature in your AI tool. By vocalizing your answers, you can say more and say it faster, and you will also provide ChatGPT with a little extra nuance that it can use to offer more specific advice when you end your response with the following prompt.

As my career coach, now that you know details about my background and my answers to these questions, what career paths or company types do you think are worth considering? Please explain why you think each suggestion could be a good next move for me.

Learn More about Suggested Paths

ChatGPT will respond with a number of suggestions based on your conversation. But this is only a starting point for you to dive deeper. If you are interested in a particular suggestion, you can ask more follow-up questions to better understand the job title and what it might take to transition your career in this direction.

Tell me more about the day-to-day responsibilities of a content marketing manager. How is it different from or similar to my current role? What additional skill sets would I need to acquire to make such a career pivot?

Pursue a Side Business

If you're looking to head off on an entrepreneurial path, ChatGPT can act as a collaborative partner in brainstorming and moving forward with a business plan uniquely catered to you. Similar to the career path exploration prompt, start by answering a series of questions from ChatGPT, then seek recommendations, and see how it translates your goals, interests, and skills into potential business ideas.

> I want to start a side business that can potentially grow into a bigger opportunity for me down the road. I would like you to recommend 5 potential business ideas that I can start from home or online, with a brief outline of how I would get started generating income in the first 3 months for each idea. Before we begin, I would like you to ask me 20 questions about my passions, motivations, background, values, strengths, and weaknesses—anything that will help you make recommendations that fit my unique interests and skills.

EXPAND YOUR NETWORK

How AI Can Help You Network

Across most career paths, networking is widely regarded as one of the most beneficial things you can do to move your career forward. If you are actively working on expanding your network, ChatGPT can help you ensure your networking conversations are both meaningful and packed with value.

When someone in your network connects you with someone else, having a memorable conversation that helps you get to know, understand, and learn from that new person can have a potentially life-changing impact on your career. With ChatGPT's help, you can generate a list of questions that can thoughtfully balance curiosity, learning, exploration, flattery, and your personal goals so that you can network effectively.

Set Up Your Initial Request

In your prompt, provide as much information as possible on who you will be speaking with. A copy + paste of the contents of their LinkedIn profile can be helpful, as well as a summary of how you connected with them. In addition, provide some details about your own background and what you are hoping to gain from this conversation. Are you seeking advice on a career transition? Searching for a job, ideally at their company? Looking for opportunities to collaborate or sell to them in the future? No matter your goals, ChatGPT can guide you to conducting an interesting, rather than tedious, conversation and hopefully making a connection for life.

Sample Starter Prompt

I have recently connected with an alumnus from my college who is the CTO of a large tech company. I am an early-career technical program manager, and I aspire to be a leader myself one day. We have a 30-minute call scheduled, and I want to make this conversation as meaningful and memorable as possible, for both of us.

Can you help me come up with a list of 15 specific, impactful, and interesting questions I should ask on our call so I can learn, seem impressive to her, and hopefully open doors for further connections? Please list them in the recommended order and explain your thought process for the recommendations.

Additional Ways to Personalize

Create a Guide to Effective Networking Practices

If networking does not come easily to you, you can turn to AI for guidance on countless situations to help you learn best practices or prepare for networking events. By including details on the "blockers" in your networking process, you can get more personalized advice.

Tomorrow I am going to a large networking event for my school's alumni. I want to expand my network at this event, but I am naturally shy and get very bored and annoyed with small talk. Please give me actionable advice for overcoming my holdups and making meaningful professional connections.

Give me specific advice for approaching new people and also gracefully exiting conversations, including 10 phrases I can turn to in a pinch for intros and exits.

Draft Outreach on LinkedIn

Reaching out to someone you are connected with but do not know well, or even someone that you do not know at all, can be a challenging task. What do you say? And how do you say it so that they respond favorably? Outreach like this, especially on LinkedIn, can lead to great new connections, new jobs, and even (if you are in sales) a closed deal. When provided with the right context, goal, and requested tone of voice, ChatGPT can save you time and stress in drafting an outreach message. Helpful context to add to your prompt includes: (1) Your relationship to this person (if any), and (2) If you and this person have anything in common.

> I need help drafting an outreach message to someone I do not know personally, but we did both attend the University of Michigan's business school. A role in finance was recently posted at their current company that I'd like to apply to, but I'm hoping they'd be willing to chat with me about their experience at the company (they work in the marketing department) and (hopefully) would be willing to refer me to the role or connect me with the hiring manager. Help me draft 3 approaches to a friendly, professional, short, and sweet LinkedIn outreach message. These should be no more than 100 words each.

ELEVATE YOUR PROFESSIONAL BRAND ON LINKEDIN

How AI Can Help You Grow a Following on LinkedIn

In addition to being a great place to network and find new job opportunities, LinkedIn has become a go-to for many people to develop their professional brand and become a thought leader in their area of expertise. Whether you are hoping to transition into the world of a professional speaker or panelist on your specialty, develop a new business idea as an entrepreneur, or promote your personal brand and ideas to attract companies and recruiters, AI tools can help you ideate and perfect thought leadership content for your LinkedIn profile.

Set Up Your Initial Request

Start by saying what primary topics you would like to talk about on LinkedIn. You should also include your qualifications, background, and details about your belief system and goals when it comes to your content. With this context, ChatGPT will be able to help you draft post ideas for your profile to which you can add the finishing touches.

Sample Starter Prompt

I am a human resources leader hoping to have a stronger presence on LinkedIn to develop my professional brand and position myself for exciting job opportunities or speaking events. I am passionate about diversity, equity, and inclusion, promoting healthy work-life balance for employees, and fostering cultures of innovation. Help me brainstorm a list of 20 content ideas for short ~150-word posts on LinkedIn that share my perspective, highlight emerging trends in my industry, and offer practical advice to businesses on how they should approach people and culture.

Additional Ways to Personalize

Use Your Own LinkedIn Writing As Training

While you can ask ChatGPT to draft content for you, you can ultimately save time editing ChatGPT's drafts by providing existing posts written in your own voice as examples of your writing style. By posting the contents of 5 to 10 LinkedIn posts you are proud of, ChatGPT can recognize the patterns in your language or formatting to guide its future post drafts.

Below are 5 examples of LinkedIn posts that I've written in the past that my audience greatly enjoyed. I need an analysis of what they have in common when it comes to tone, style, and structure. Then use that analysis to guide your future drafts to be similar to these posts. Here they are: (1) <paste 1> (2) <paste 2> (3) <paste 3> (4) <paste 4> (5) <paste 5>.

Draft LinkedIn Posts According to Your Niche

Once you've got your ideas listed out and your writing style analyzed, you can ask ChatGPT to draft content for the post ideas it has generated in your tone of voice, using the following prompt. Keep in mind that it's best to use these samples as a first draft and refine from there to be sure everything accurately reflects your thoughts before publishing to the world!

Now draft 3 ~150-word LinkedIn posts for the idea "DEI best practices." All should start with a compelling or surprising hook so people keep reading, evolve into interesting conclusions, tell stories and share data where prudent, and end in a compelling call to action. Keep in mind my established writing style and tone in your drafts.

Get Feedback on Your Post Content

If you are drafting content on your own, or if you would just like extra feedback on what you have edited, you can ask AI to be an editor, getting advice on how you might reorder or adjust your drafted content to have even more impact on the LinkedIn platform.

Acting as an expert LinkedIn thought leader, give me actionable advice on how I might improve this draft post to gain superior engagement on LinkedIn <paste your draft>.

CREATE THOUGHTFUL INTERVIEW QUESTIONS

Hiring for a new role? Interviewing candidates is not always easy, especially if your company lacks standard processes. With ChatGPT's help, you can get advice on conducting a fair and enjoyable interview process and come up with a strong set of questions for you to ask candidates.

> I am hiring my first direct report for the associate marketing manager role and will start conducting interviews next week. I have attached the job description for reference. In addition to meeting the criteria outlined in the job description, what is very important to me is hiring someone with an inherent drive and curiosity, who is not afraid to go the extra mile and reach out to others to get the answers they need to move forward. Can you help me generate a list of 15 interview questions I might ask the candidates to determine the best fit for this role? Justify your recommendations.

GIVE CONSTRUCTIVE FEEDBACK TO A COLLEAGUE

Giving feedback to your coworkers on how you can best work with each other is essential to achieving your goals and decreasing interpersonal frustrations at work. But it's only useful when the feedback is in a format and tone that will make them more likely to receive it. This can be tough when conflict arises or when you are irritated by that person's actions or habits. ChatGPT can suggest direct feedback that is most likely to yield positive results.

> My coworker has been really annoying me with <context and details on the things that have been bothering you and things you'd like to see improve>. Can you give me some methods to format feedback to them in a way that articulates the impact this is having on me, in a way that they are most likely to receive it without becoming defensive?

EVALUATE FURTHER EDUCATIONAL OPPORTUNITIES

Choosing to pursue further education is a significant decision that often involves evaluating a lot of trade-offs, weighing the investment of time and money against the potential career outcomes from the choice. Whether you are contemplating college, graduate school, or even an online course, ChatGPT can be a great help in the decision-making process. It can also help you think about different educational focuses and weigh them against your values and desired career trajectory.

> I am a senior product manager with 8 years of experience, making $140,000 annually. I am exploring the idea of getting an MBA to advance my career, but I am concerned about the cost and return on investment considering the current salary I've achieved. Can you assist me in conducting a cost-benefit analysis, taking into account the tuition fees, potential loss of income during the program, and the expected increase in salary and career opportunities post-MBA? Please ask me whatever questions are necessary to best inform your analysis.

ANNOUNCE A PROMOTION OR CAREER MILESTONE ON LINKEDIN

Achieving a milestone is a huge accomplishment and something worth bragging about! It also lets your network keep up to date with your progress and see you as someone worthwhile to stay connected to, plus the praise that comes in from your network can give you a little boost of serotonin. Despite these benefits, many of us shy away from such announcements, worried about how others might react or simply because we're not sure how to share the news effectively. By providing ChatGPT with context on your big announcement, and your path to achieving it, you can draft an engaging post to share with your network.

> I've recently gotten a big promotion, and I would like to share this achievement with my network on LinkedIn. Here is some context <context>. Please write a concise LinkedIn post of no more than 150 words announcing my achievement. Start with a captivating introduction line and summarize my journey to tell a great story while expressing gratitude. The tone should be upbeat, positive, and humble.

LEARN NEW SKILLS FOR COMMON SOFTWARE

From learning how to write advanced formulas in Excel to better understanding the capabilities of PowerPoint, you can answer your questions and learn to do more with the software you use at work with a prompt to ChatGPT. Simply describe what you are trying to accomplish, and AI tools will provide you with suggestions or tutorials.

> In my Excel spreadsheet, I have a column of data representing daily website visitor counts over a year. I want to identify the day with the highest and lowest visitor count, identify the average visitors per day in this period, and identify the total traffic during the year. What Excel formulas do I use to find these values?

PICK UP CODING

Teaching yourself a new coding language like SQL, Python, or HTML? ChatGPT and other AI tools can not only explain programming concepts and theory; they can also help you with code examples and even debugging the code you are writing. Just treat ChatGPT like a friend already knowledgeable in these coding languages and ask for advice on a specific problem.

> I want to better understand how to write SQL code for data pulling and analysis. I'm still very much a beginner, and I only know basic commands like "select," "from," and "where." Please create a guide to learning SQL beyond these functions and clearly explain what functions are and how to format them in code.

ENHANCE YOUR WRITTEN COMMUNICATIONS

Most of us have to write in some way or another at work, whether it is writing an email to a key stakeholder, creating a project presentation, or providing written customer service. ChatGPT can be an excellent partner in your writing process, acting as a boundless thesaurus or an idea generator for phrasing, naming, copywriting, or creating slide presentation headlines.

> Here is the current title of a slide in my company's pitch deck: "<paste in title>." It's too long and not very compelling. The slide talks about <summary of what it discusses>. Help me come up with 10 different titles that help introduce this slide. The tone should be inspirational and compelling.

BRAINSTORM ALTERNATIVE APPROACHES

AI tools make for excellent brainstorming partners because of their vast training data and ability to recognize patterns and synthesize ideas and perspectives across a wide range of topics almost instantaneously. If you are stuck and in need of additional ideas for a work-related issue, simply give ChatGPT some background on the problem you are trying to solve as well as any constraints you have in solving the problem, and ask for 5 to 10 alternative ideas or approaches.

I market a tool that helps teach elementary schoolkids foreign languages. It can run on tablets and desktops. While kids are the main users, parents have to sign up. We have been trying to get our product into schools more effectively but are having little luck. Could you give me 5 distinct and different ideas to increase interest from schools for this product?

CHAPTER 6

Personal Finance and Financial Literacy

According to MarketWatch Guides, as of May 2024, only 57% of Americans are financially literate. If you never had a dedicated class on money management or investing in school, and if your family or friends don't regularly share ideas and advice about money, it has probably been up to you to find answers on your own…if you even know what to look for. When it comes to personal finance, you often just don't know what you don't know. And the time it takes to dig through Google searches or read books on money management is a luxury you probably don't have.

AI can help bridge knowledge gaps in your financial literacy, introducing new topics, answering questions quickly in an approachable way, and helping you learn at your own pace. Beyond teaching you about new financial concepts, these tools can also help you act on this new knowledge, from outlining a personalized budget, to evaluating company financials for investing, to acting as a personal financial coach, and more. In this chapter, you'll learn how AI can help you on your financial journey and uncover even more topics to dive into through its responses!

OPTIMIZE YOUR BUDGET

How AI Can Help You Build a Better Budget

Understanding your income and the best way to allocate it is one of the best ways to start practicing good financial habits. According to NerdWallet, however, nearly one in four Americans keep no budget at all, and of those who do, 84% admit they've sometimes exceeded that budget.

A good budgeting practice will make you conscious of your means and keep you from overspending. Whether you are new to budgeting or have had trouble in the past sticking to your budget, AI can help by acting as your financial coach.

Set Up Your Initial Request

In your first prompt, share with ChatGPT as much about your current situation as you are comfortable with. What is your monthly income? How much do you have in savings? Are there any goals you are trying to achieve by budgeting better, like paying off debt or building an emergency fund? Provide whatever detail you have readily available, and you can fill in anything you miss with ChatGPT's follow-up questions, which you can answer quickly by leveraging the voice-to-text feature.

Sample Starter Prompt

I need your help establishing a better monthly budgeting practice to reduce overspending and grow my savings. After taxes, I bring home about $4,200 a month, about $1,700 of which is spent on monthly bills, rent, and car payments. After I pay $200/month in student loans, I generally only have $100 left over at the end of each month. I have about $4,000 in savings, but I would like to get to $10,000 for an emergency fund. Ask me up to 5 questions to allow you to ultimately guide me through a more personalized budgeting strategy and create better goals for my savings and categorical spending.

Unpack Your Money Mindset

After you have answered ChatGPT's follow-up questions, it will provide some suggestions for you to consider and even a sample budget breakdown if you request it. With this information, you might want to examine your behaviors and feelings around money to guide you through overcoming obstacles in your budgeting journey.

Acting as a financial coach, help me unpack any psychological tendencies I have toward spending or saving by asking me a series of questions to help me better approach my finances.

Recommend New Budgeting Frameworks

If you have traditionally had trouble sticking to a budget, your approach may be partially to blame. ChatGPT can introduce you to a variety of methods people have used to successfully budget, and explain to you how these methods work, which would be a good fit for you, and why. Want to dig deeper into any particular framework? Just ask ChatGPT to "tell you more" about it and how you might apply it!

Recommend multiple proven budgeting frameworks, with an explanation of what they are, why they work, and why they might be helpful to my situation.

Create a Plan for Monthly Reflection

Establishing a regular practice of reflecting on your finances and spending can help you reach your goals faster and stay mindful of your progress. You can leverage AI to suggest recommended routines and reflection questions. From there, on a monthly basis, you can even come back to the same chat and detail information on your progress as well as your reflections, to which ChatGPT will continue to respond as an encouraging coach.

I want to establish a better practice of reviewing and reflecting on my expenses and overall financial health so I can be more conscious of my spending habits and progress into a place of more financial stability. Please create a monthly exercise I can conduct in less than an hour to help me critically assess my expenses, including 5 essential questions to reflect on each month.

BOOST YOUR SAVINGS

How AI Can Help You Save More Money

Whether you are trying to cut back on your spending or you just enjoy finding a good deal, ChatGPT and other AI tools can not only inform you of creative and little-known ways to save on common purchases; they can also help you determine the best time to buy various items on your shopping list.

Set Up Your Initial Request

There are countless ways to save money across various spending categories, especially in the digital world. Start with a broad approach using ChatGPT to uncover new ideas that you can explore in more depth in subsequent prompts. Start by detailing what specific spending categories take up the largest portion of your wallet and request little-known tips and recommendations for consumer product savings that you could leverage.

Sample Starter Prompt

Acting as an expert in frugal living and sourcing the best deals, create a robust guide to saving money on common necessities, like household bills, car expenses and transportation, clothing, medication, and groceries. Include secret tips and tricks that many do not know. Finally, for each category, list any consumer apps or tech that may provide further discounts in each category.

Additional Ways to Personalize

Learn the Right Time to Buy

If you can afford to wait a little while to purchase an item on your list, you might be able to save a good bit of money. ChatGPT can create a guide to purchases with lower prices at certain times of the year or help you determine the best time of year to consider purchasing a specific item on your list.

Create a table detailing 40 types of items and the times of year it is best to purchase them to get the best price. The columns should be "Item," "Times of Year," and "Reasoning." The final column explains why the price is typically best at that time.

Learn Where Sales Are Honored Post-Purchase

Have you ever purchased something at full price only to discover that it went on sale just days later? Many stores honor price decreases within a certain time frame after your purchase is made. Before your next online shopping spree or trip to the mall, use AI to make a rapid breakdown of stores and their post-purchase policies around sales so you know how long you should watch for a price drop on that must-have item after you purchase it.

Create a table detailing 20 consumer stores selling clothing that honor sale prices if you purchase something that later goes on sale. The columns should be "Store" and "Time Frame" (in what time frame after purchase is the sale price honored).

Get Tips for Savvy Online Shopping

If you do most of your shopping online, and you aren't always getting some kind of discount, ask AI for help. There is usually a discount to be found if only you know where and how to look for it! ChatGPT can make a quick guide of tips that you can implement the next time you "Add to Cart."

Acting as an experienced deal finder, make a robust guide to 20 ways to secure the best discounts when shopping online, including little-known tips and tricks.

Research Banking Options for Your Savings

Building your savings is key to financial health, but savings set aside in a bank account won't do nearly as much for your finances if they are earning interest rates lower than the annual rate of inflation. AI tools with web-browsing capabilities can help you learn ways to make your savings work for you and rapidly research what options are available on the market.

I want to do more with my savings and emergency fund, which are currently earning a low 0.05% annual percentage yield. Help me find the best options available on the market right now for savings accounts or neobanks with high annual percentage yield, or certificates of deposit for periods of 12 months or less. Please also detail anything else I should be considering and how to think through where I allocate my savings.

NEGOTIATE LARGE EXPENSES

How AI Can Help You Secure a Better Price

Spending a little extra time and effort negotiating the price of a major purchase can save you a lot of money in the long run. Still, not many people feel comfortable negotiating or may not even know that negotiation is acceptable or even expected in certain scenarios. By leaning on ChatGPT as a negotiation coach, you can not only learn about when it is appropriate and worthwhile to negotiate but also how to most effectively go about it.

Set Up Your Initial Request

If you are new to negotiating, it can be helpful to get a loose understanding of what things are commonly negotiable and also learn the basics of how to effectively negotiate. ChatGPT can summarize the contents of books on negotiation by using reviews and discussions to create an indirect summary on the subject. The details can inspire you on how much you stand to save when you take the time to negotiate.

Sample Starter Prompt

Make a comprehensive guide to effective negotiation, summarizing widespread techniques and frameworks from popular books on the subject. In your guide, additionally include 10 unique things that are negotiable but are rarely negotiated. Provide any information on what one could manage to save on these items if they negotiated.

Additional Ways to Personalize

Negotiate a New Car Purchase
Negotiation is a huge part of the car purchasing process, but it can be arduous, especially if you are doing it for the first time or you simply prefer to avoid

it. ChatGPT can help you break down all the tactics of successful negotiation and provide added guidance on the best time to buy or what research to conduct to make the process a little less painful.

> Outline strategies for negotiating the price of a new car purchased from a dealership. Include detailed information on all levers I might pull to secure the best price possible in my negotiation. For each lever, include tactics and resources for securing the appropriate information, as well as tips for broaching the subjects confidently with the dealer.

Prepare and Set Expectations for Large Medical Expenses

Medical procedures can often result in a variety of unexpected costs, but there are several proactive steps you can take to both set expectations and make choices that may reduce the ultimate expense. With ChatGPT, you don't need to know all of the nuances of the medical billing system to make a plan and feel prepared. Detail the procedure you need to have and the country it will take place in, and request information breaking down unexpected costs and how to reduce them.

> I am pregnant and nervous about the inevitable medical cost of giving birth, having heard stories where hospital visits result in high unexpected costs. Please give me an idea of the potential costs associated with childbirth. Then create a comprehensive guide to avoiding unexpected costs as a woman in America with health insurance. For each piece of advice, provide specifics on what to do and how to negotiate to pay the lowest cost after being billed.

Get Tips for Negotiating Large Medical Bills

Now that you've gotten a breakdown of what to do before your medical procedure to save on costs, ask ChatGPT break down tips for further negotiating or reducing costs for the specific scenario after the procedure has taken place. From there, ask follow-up questions on items detailed in your guide to dive deeper into how best to execute the advice.

Now provide me with detailed guidance on negotiating or reducing the cost of my hospital bills after I have given birth, including little-known tips that can save a lot of money.

Practice Negotiation Directly

Feeling nervous about your upcoming negotiation? Leverage ChatGPT's voice functionality to practice an out-loud negotiation ahead of time. In your prompt, lay out the negotiation scenario you are going to enter, providing details on the role it should be playing and how difficult it may be to negotiate with. As you progress through the role-play, you can even ask for ChatGPT to break character and provide advice on the previous conversation as to what you can do better.

I need your help practicing for an upcoming negotiation to purchase a new car. You are to play the role of the salesperson at the car dealership. You are polite and reasonable, and your goal is to try to maintain as much profit as possible while also addressing my concerns and counteroffers and ultimately selling the car. Here are some details on the scenario: <detail specifics on what you are purchasing, any details on rates, or background details on negotiations you've already had or add-ons the dealer is trying to push>. I will start the negotiation, and I would like you to respond as a salesperson might in real life as we negotiate.

PREPARE YOUR TAXES

How AI Can Help You with Taxes

The federal tax system is incredibly complex and can vary from state to state and from year to year. In fact, a recent Pew Research study revealed that 85% of Americans experience at least some frustration with the tax system's complexity. A better understanding of the tax system, while daunting, can be very advantageous—you'll have a sense of how changes in the tax code will impact you and what pretax selections from your employer you might consider taking advantage of.

Of course, generative AI tools are *not* certified public accountants, but they can provide accurate information on these topics at no cost and in a timely manner so that you know how to search for more details or what to ask a CPA the next time you meet. Leverage tools with access to web browsing for the best chance at accuracy, and once you've got some ideas, you can find all the specifics at a trusted source like IRS.gov.

Set Up Your Initial Request

When using ChatGPT to level up your understanding of the tax system, it's helpful to start with some foundational knowledge on how you might optimize your taxes ahead of the filing season. Start by giving ChatGPT relevant information on how you earn money then asking it to make a robust guide to reducing your tax liability.

Sample Starter Prompt

Create a guide on 15–25 proactive ways I can reduce my tax liability as a W-2 employee in the United States who also runs a side business selling baked goods on Etsy.

Dive Deeper Into Tax-Saving Strategies

Once you have your guide, continue to ask in follow-up prompts for more details on how to execute these actions for the upcoming tax year and if there are any limitations or qualifications you may need to meet to be eligible.

Tell me more about <suggestion> and any limitations or qualifications I should consider for the tax year <year>. Keep your answers specific to my situation.

Understand Your Tax Liability

If you've ever taken a look at your pay stub and wondered, "Where did all my money go?" or "How was this calculated?" AI can help you quickly break it down. This can be particularly helpful for individuals with mixed streams of income to better understand what their tax liability will likely be come tax season, or for anyone considering a new job offer (perhaps in another state) who wants to understand how their take-home income will be affected. For this query, I recommend using ChatGPT's data analytics feature for more accuracy on the exact math. But asking any model to explain its process will also help you to fact-check the accuracy of the math the model produces.

Calculate approximately what I will owe in income taxes, state taxes, social security, and Medicare if I am a single W-2 employee in Alabama making $90,000 a year in salary in 2024 and $10,000 annually through self-employment. Explain your process and calculations.

Understand How Changes in the Tax Code Impact You

When you hear about changes to the federal income tax brackets, you may wonder how these changes impact your tax liability. Leveraging ChatGPT's data analytics and web-browsing capabilities will help you to rapidly break down the estimated impact on your taxes owed in the next year.

What are the current income tax brackets in <current tax year>, and have they adjusted at all compared to <previous tax year>? How will this impact the taxes I pay given that my W-2 salary is <salary>? Please clearly break down what I owed in <previous year> compared to what I will owe in <current year>.

Get Guidance on the Best Business Structure to Use for Your Business

If you have recently started a business that generates side income, congratulations! With the help of AI, you can quickly learn about the benefits and drawbacks of different potential business structures for your business—for example, sole proprietorships versus LLCs versus S corporations. You can also figure out how each type will impact your tax obligations. For the most personalized recommendation, include details in your prompt about your business's income as well as any additional income you earn.

I am trying to understand the differences between the various structures I could choose for my side business, which has started to earn consistent earnings. Please make a detailed guide showing the differences between and pros and cons of (1) a sole proprietorship, (2) an LLC, and (3) an S corporation. Detail under what scenarios each business structure is most useful and highlight specifically how each of these structures can impact the taxes I may owe. As additional context, my side business has made $20,000 in the first 2 months of this year alone, and I expect this to grow. I also earn a $110,000 salary as a W-2 employee at my day job.

Understand Tax Deductibility of Side-Business Expenses

Social security tax is typically higher on income earned by the self-employed, and qualified deductions are a great way to reduce your overall liability while also reinvesting in your business. With ChatGPT you can learn about what deductions may or may not qualify for your business to help you understand which receipts are worth saving. Provide ChatGPT with some details about your business, then describe the expense, asking if it could be deducted.

> I have a side business baking and selling baked goods on Etsy. I use social media to promote my business, and I recently made an Instagram Reel about my process of re-creating some pastries I've purchased from Starbucks, which I feature in the video. Could these pastries used in the video be tax deductible? If so, how would I itemize that in my taxes?

BUY A HOME

How AI Can Aid the Home-Buying Process

The home-buying process, especially if you are taking part in it for the first time, can be exciting but also overwhelming. During the search process, you'll need to consider many factors (both financial and emotional) that will impact you for years to come. While you can't beat having a great real estate agent to help you along the way, AI can serve as an always-on guide from the beginning (even before you've secured that agent!). From helping you understand the process, the associated costs, and your financial readiness for it to supporting you as you sort through observations from your home tours, AI can help you move through the process with confidence and clarity.

Set Up Your Initial Request

If you have never bought a home before, the overall process and associated costs can seem very complicated and come with surprises if you are not prepared. Before you dive in, ChatGPT can provide you with a clear overview of the steps you can expect as well as an estimate of all the costs associated with the home-buying process and early home ownership.

I am thinking about buying a home soon, but I am not familiar with all the associated costs and processes. Please break down the home-buying process (from where I am now to the final purchase) and include cost estimates on what I need to be financially prepared for when purchasing a home and in the first few years of home ownership.

Additional Ways to Personalize ─●

Evaluate Financial Readiness for Home Ownership

When you are preparing for a home search, it is important to look at your finances holistically. This will help you feel prepared for the upcoming costs and understand how the purchase price of a home may impact your financial situation in the long run. ChatGPT can guide you through evaluating your finances for a potential future home purchase and give you a sense of how different home prices may impact your lifestyle given the current mortgage rates.

I would like you to evaluate my financial situation to help me determine if I am financially ready for home ownership and determine what price of home is reasonable for my financial situation. Ask me 5 questions to kick off this evaluation. Once I've answered, share your conclusions before asking more questions to dive deeper.

Document Your Home Search

Searching for your first home can be exciting and anxiety-inducing. In a single week, you'll visit countless homes with different price points, quirks, pros, and cons. It can be exhausting to remember all the details of what you learn in a quick tour. When you use ChatGPT in your home search, you'll unlock an always-there secretary to document and summarize your thoughts as you go! Prime your chat with instructions, then as you visit each home, speak your thoughts out loud using voice-to-text.

Today I am looking at a variety of houses that I am considering buying. I need you to act as my secretary. Throughout the day, I will leave you a bunch of rambling notes about my observations and opinions on different homes, which I need you to clearly summarize. At the end of my search, I will ask you to evaluate all the different homes to compare them. I will assign each home a number or a name (like a street name). Let's start with home number one on Clancy Avenue. Here are my observations: <detail everything you'd like to remember about the home, the price, the location, etc.>.

Summarize Your Home Tours

At the end of your day or weekend of visiting homes, you can leverage your chat history within ChatGPT to neatly summarize your observations across homes. ChatGPT can also uncover pearls of wisdom hidden within your rambled observations that may help you in determining what homes to seriously consider as favorites for a potential purchase.

I need you to clearly summarize the pros and cons of all the homes I looked at today, and, based on what you have learned from listening to me, please point out if there are any homes you think I may be leaning toward and why.

SELL YOUR STUFF

How AI Can Help You Sell Your Unwanted Items

Most of us have extra stuff hanging around the house. If you've decided it's time to declutter, AI can help you list your items for resale online and turn clutter into cash with a fraction of the upfront time investment on your part. With ChatGPT, you can get guidance on where to sell and how to price your items, and even write search-optimized descriptions for your listings.

Set Up Your Initial Request

If you've got items that you are ready to sell, start by having ChatGPT create a detailed guide to the best online marketplaces to sell these items. In your prompt, detail what your primary motivators are (getting rid of stuff quickly, no matter the earnings? Making as much as possible for your items?) and include what kinds of items you are hoping to sell.

Sample Starter Prompt

I'm hoping to resell a number of things, including luxury clothing and accessories, furniture, used electronics, and some collectibles. Make a guide breaking down different online marketplaces for resellers like me to consider selling these items, breaking down the pros and cons of each, and detailing what types of items are best to sell on which platforms. My top priority is securing a fair or good selling price and simple setup, as I am new to this.

Additional Ways to Personalize

Create a Guide to Selling on a Particular Website

Once you've learned which marketplace may be best for the items you are trying to sell, your AI tool can guide you on how to open a seller account on this platform and effectively list products.

I'd like to learn more about selling my <item type> on <name of online marketplace>. Create a detailed step-by-step guide with clear advice and advanced tips for how to most effectively sell on this platform and secure the best purchase price.

Get Suggestions for Listing Prices

Not quite sure what a fair price is for a particular item? An AI with web-browsing capabilities can provide you with suggestions on a listing price range that you might want to target for trickier items like antiques or collectibles. In your prompt, provide as much detail as you can on the product—the brand, the year it was made, or the condition, for example.

I have an original still-in-the-box 1963 Easy-Bake Oven. I want to understand its value if I were to sell it. Approximate its value and give me a complete list of the criteria that would make it more or less valuable. Please also provide comparable listings for this item for me to review.

Write Detailed Product Listings

For the best chance of selling your items online, it is important to have a well-written and compelling description thoroughly describing the item and include important keywords and phrases so that your listing actually shows up when someone is searching for it. Doing this on your own can be very time-consuming, but with ChatGPT's help, you can write a fully optimized listing in just a few minutes.

I need your help writing a detailed product listing for <name of item> on <name of platform>, optimized for keywords that someone who might want to buy this product would search for. In your description, include all necessary elements of the product listing for this platform (name, description, tags if used by the platform, etc.).

LEARN HOW TO INVEST

How AI Can Help You with Investing

Most financial advisors will tell you that investing is instrumental to building long-term wealth. Through the power of compounding, wise investments can outpace inflation over time and grow well beyond what your money might have done just sitting in a bank account. Even if you recognize that investing is a smart thing to do, the prospect of starting to invest can seem daunting. Where and how should you start investing? What can you even invest in? If you've ever found yourself pondering these questions, you're in luck: with AI, it's easy to learn all about investing at a pace that's right for you.

Set Up Your Initial Request

One of the biggest barriers to knowledge growth can simply be not knowing what questions to ask. To get a clear understanding of all the various topics to learn on the subject of investing, I recommend you start by asking ChatGPT to make a sample course outline on investing. Once you understand what there is to ask about, leverage topics from your "course" to create more robust guides on any investing subject.

Sample Starter Prompt

I am totally new to investing, other than knowing that it is a good thing to do to grow my long-term wealth. I need you to create a robust course outline on the subject of investing titled "Investing: From Beginning to Expert." In this course, start with the basics of investing knowledge and progress into expert-level education on the subject of investing, covering all different types of investments and investment accounts.

Go Deeper Into Topics from Your Course Outline

Now that you have a lengthy list of investing-related topics from your course outline to reference, you need only ask within the same chat for a more thorough breakdown of concepts for any particular subject matter.

> Please write a guide to Section 3.2 of the investing course you have just created, "Fundamental Analysis," explained in a way I can easily understand as someone new to investing.

Learn about Different Investing Accounts

When you have a finite amount of money that you can set aside for investments, it is wise to consider what kinds of accounts best suit your particular situation and goals. In your prompt, detail your goal for investing. For example, are you aiming to retire, investing for a large purchase in future years, or saving for your child's education? Then ask ChatGPT to break down how you might optimize your investment accounts for your goals.

> Acting as a seasoned financial advisor, create a guide to the different types of investment accounts, particularly those that can be leveraged in retirement, and in what priority order I should consider opening them to set me up for the best financial outcomes in the long term. Include details on the relative pros and cons for each of these account types to consider.

Understand the Differences Between Investment Assets

Just as there are a variety of types of investment accounts, there are also countless asset types in which one can invest. ChatGPT can help you understand these different options, how you might evaluate them, and their relative risks.

Provide me with a detailed guide to the differences among all the varied types of investment assets, including bonds, ETFs, CDs, stocks, and any other types of alternative assets I may not be mentioning. Detail their relative level of risk, how they work, and what to consider when purchasing these assets.

Get Guidance Evaluating Stocks for Purchase

While investing in individual stocks is typically riskier than choosing a diversified fund, the rewards with a well-researched stock purchase can be higher. To make a strong purchase decision, though, you should research, explore a company's financials, and understand its performance compared to others in that industry. With the help of AI, you can learn the processes by which experienced investors evaluate stocks for purchase.

Create a guide to effectively evaluating a stock for purchase in the stock market, including details on how to interpret all key information about the stock. Provide guidance on how I might compare one type of asset against another in order to make an informed purchase decision.

Evaluate Company Financial Statements

AI tools can also expedite all of your research processes. Be sure to use an AI tool with web access for summarizing recent news and PDF attachment capabilities to review recent company financial statements. These tools can also summarize information from analysts on how others expect the stocks to perform.

Attached are the public earnings statements between 4 quarters for AAPL stock. Please evaluate these statements and share your observations about the changes over time for this stock and how those changes might be interpreted regarding the performance of this stock over time.

Summarize Analyst Sentiment on a Stock

By leveraging an AI tool with web-browsing capabilities, you can also rapidly summarize what analysts are currently predicting for any stock's performance. If you include the word *currently* or a phrase like *in the past few weeks*, this signals ChatGPT to leverage web browsing. The output will also include hyperlinks to sources for further reading.

Please summarize what analysts are currently saying about AAPL and whether it is a "buy" or "sell." Include details on price targets and ratings, reasons for the sentiment, and any concerns or risks.

CREATE A PERSONALIZED FINANCIAL PLAN

If you are comfortable with sharing detailed financial information with an AI tool, you can get deeply personalized suggestions for how to approach financial decisions, like paying off debt or making a major purchase. Simply ask ChatGPT to engage with you while acting as a financial advisor. If you already document your financials somewhere, like in a spreadsheet, you can even attach this in your prompt as context. Just remember: Never share sensitive information like credit card or bank account numbers.

> I would like you to engage with me acting as a seasoned financial advisor. I have attached a document detailing my current financial situation. At this time, I am most focused on paying off my debt, but I also know I should be thinking about my future as well. Keeping in mind the details of my current situation, what should I consider in my approach as a part of my larger future financial plan? Please ask me up to 5 additional questions that may help you advise me on my financial journey.

RESEARCH MAJOR PURCHASES

When making major purchases like a new car or an expensive appliance, conducting research ahead of time can help you find the best offering that fits your needs and your budget. But understanding product specifications and scrolling through customer reviews can take a significant amount of time. AI tools, especially those with web-browsing capabilities, can help expedite the process by creating comparative charts, summarizing publicly available customer reviews online, and providing information on the things you should be considering when making a purchase decision.

> My family is in the market for a new refrigerator and would ideally like to spend no more than $2,000, including estimated taxes and delivery costs. We require a fridge-plus-freezer that is less than 35 inches wide and prefer one with a bottom freezer.
> Please make an in-depth comparison chart of 10 top-rated refrigerators within our budget at a wide range of price points. Highlight the estimated price point, the dimensions of the fridge, what customers like and dislike

about each, the value for the money, and a description of differentiating features. My goal is to get the best refrigerator for the price point and one that has a long lifespan relative to the cost.

EVALUATE COST OF LIVING VS. SALARY

Understanding the cost of living in a given locale relative to your income can be critical in your decision-making. AI can quickly help you make a cost-of-living analysis for different cities you are considering and also guide you in making an informed decision when you provide more detail on your overall goals with the move or new position. It can even suggest neighborhoods to consider renting in, with details on the "why" behind each one!

> I'm considering 2 job offers: one in Austin, Texas, with a salary of $70,000, and the other in San Francisco, California, with a salary of $82,000. I need your help comparing the cost of living (transportation, food, gas, etc.) and average rent prices for a one-bedroom apartment within a 30-minute commute of the downtown area in each city. I need you to estimate how these costs will impact my budget and lifestyle, considering the salaries offered, and make an informed recommendation around which job might make sense to choose and why, all other things about the job considered equal. Finally, for both cities, I would like you to recommend 5 neighborhoods I might consider renting in that are considered safe, enjoyable, and affordable for a 20-something new to the city. For each neighborhood, explain your recommendation.

GUIDE DEBT-REDUCTION STRATEGIES

In January 2024, Bankrate reported that nearly half (49%) of American credit card holders carried their credit card debt month to month on at least one card. To make matters worse, the average interest rate on cards was more than 20%. Paying off debt, especially at high interest rates, is not easy. But there are a variety of strategic ways to reduce debt, and with ChatGPT as a partner, you can set yourself on a clearer path to being debt-free.

Acting as a financial advisor with 20 years of experience, create an in-depth, clear, and well-organized guide to effective debt consolidation and proven repayment strategies for someone with significant debt across multiple credit cards and student loans. Include ultra-specific tips and considerations for every part of the plan.

LEARN ABOUT DIFFERENT TYPES OF INSURANCE

There are countless kinds of insurance out there, and so many nuances in coverage and rates across them all. Most insurance policies require a monthly premium, which you'll want to compare from company to company. ChatGPT can help you understand the whole process, from teaching you the differences between types of insurance to guiding you through policy selection. Here are some prompt examples for evaluating and understanding both life and health insurance plans.

I need your help to better understand life insurance and whether it would be a good decision to purchase it now. First, clearly explain all the differences between "whole life insurance" and "term life insurance" and the pros and cons of each. Detail under what situations it is useful to consider purchasing life insurance, then ask me 10 questions to help evaluate if doing so is the best choice for me right now.

Attached are documents detailing the different healthcare plans I'm evaluating to cover myself, my husband, and my 2 children. Could you help me understand the key differences among these plans when it comes to the associated costs and the coverage provided? Please also explain to me very clearly what the differences are and what they mean (for example: co-pay, deductibles, out-of-pocket maximums, the network options) and any unique benefits of any of the plan options. Could you also provide insights on how these differences might affect me based on a broad range of healthcare needs? I'm looking for an analysis that will help me interpret the pros and cons of each plan to make an informed decision.

UNDERSTAND HOW CREDIT SCORES WORK

Maintaining or building a good credit score can have a huge impact on your life and save you a lot of money in the long run. A strong credit score can increase the likelihood of being approved for housing rentals, give you access to higher borrowing limits, and even make you seem like a better hire for certain jobs than someone with a lower credit score. A strong credit score can also help you secure lower interest rates on loans, from mortgages to car payments, saving you thousands of dollars in the long run. Understanding how credit scores are calculated is an effective first step to building a better one, and AI can help you bridge that knowledge gap.

> Acting as an expert financial advisor, create a robust learning guide to understanding credit scores in America. What is a credit score? How is it calculated? Are there different types of scores? What are all of the factors that can raise or lower a score? These are the types of questions I'd like answered, in deep detail.

GET ADVICE ON IMPROVING YOUR CREDIT SCORE

Many Americans are woefully undereducated about how they can improve their credit scores. According to a Capital One Insights Center survey, over a third of Americans falsely believe that carrying a balance on their credit card each month *improves* their credit score. Lack of knowledge is actively harming many of us financially, but with AI, you can unpack myths and get actionable guidance on steps to improving your credit score.

> Give me a step-by-step guide to improving my credit score. Include suggestions on the order in which to do things and explain your thought process. If there are little-known ways to increase my credit score, include those as well. Please also provide me with 10 common false assumptions about credit scores and share why they are misguided so that I can avoid false traps.

RESEARCH CREDIT CARD SIGN-UP BONUSES

For those who use them wisely, credit cards can offer great benefits that make them worthwhile to use for spending instead of a debit card or cash. From cash back, to huge sign-up bonuses, to travel insurance and more, the offerings on the market are wide and varied. When it comes to credit card perks, AI tools with web-browsing capabilities can not only help you rapidly research some of the best on the market, but they can also help you discover those offering particularly strong signup bonuses!

> I'm in the market for a new credit card. Make a guide to personal credit cards on the market right now with strong sign-up bonus offers. These can be in points or cash, but for points, include the approximate cash value. For each card you recommend, detail the interest rate, other major card perks, any annual fees, and cash-back structure. Include at least 10 cards.

SUMMARIZE YOUR CREDIT CARD BENEFITS

If used wisely, credit cards can open up a world of enjoyable perks and benefits, from discounted travel to covered subscription services and significant cash back across different categories. But with so many benefits, it can be hard to keep track of everything and know which card is best to put what charges on! By leveraging an AI with web browsing, you can get a quick understanding of the perks across your "credit card portfolio" and make sure you are taking advantage of them.

> I need your help researching and breaking down the benefits across all of my credit cards. I have a Capital One SavorOne Rewards Card, a Citi Double Cash Card, and an Amex Platinum Card. Detail a full list of all perks (cash back, subscriptions/memberships, credits, etc.) and rewards currently included for each of these cards and suggest how I should optimize my spending across categories to these cards for the highest cash-back amounts and savings.

CHAPTER 7

Personal Growth and Learning

"**W**hen you are finished changing, you're finished." This thought-provoking quote is most often attributed to Benjamin Franklin, whose belief in constant personal development and lifelong learning led him to not only be a founding father of the United States but also to make remarkable scientific discoveries, inventions, and innovations that still influence us today. But not all of us can apply a similar level of rigor to our development in the busy modern world…at least, not without the right support.

Whether you're guided by a New Year's resolution or a deeper determination to change your life, ChatGPT and similar tools can help you with every step along the way, from goal setting and plan forming to learning and reflection. AI's vast set of training data combined with its incredible ability to comprehend conversation means that you can bridge your knowledge gap on countless subjects in a manner that best matches your learning style. You can also engage with ChatGPT as you would a coach, teacher, or trusted friend to help you carve out a clear path for any of your personal development goals.

While I can't promise you that ChatGPT will lead you to the same level of history-making fame as Ben Franklin, I can assure you that with AI's help, you can accomplish more goals and develop into an even better version of yourself. In this chapter, we'll unpack some of the countless ways you can use ChatGPT and other AI tools to help you set and achieve goals, learn more efficiently, think through problems better, and develop into the best version of you!

BECOME YOUR LIFE COACH

How AI Can Help You As a Coach and Mentor

The hustle and bustle of daily life can sometimes drag us down, distract us, and cause us to lose sight of our goals and dreams, as well as our path to accomplishing them. For some, the solution is to hire a life coach to guide them through goal setting and personal development paths while offering them perspective, support, and encouragement.

But a good life coach can charge hundreds of dollars an hour. Meanwhile, AI tools, although lacking the human element *real-life* coaches can offer, can deliver a lot of suggestions and encouragement while being free and fast. By prompting AI to act as your life coach, these tools can help you home in on what matters most to you, set effective goals that align with your life mission, and come up with a plan to reach them.

Set Up Your Initial Request

Start with a reflective request, sharing details about your current situation, as well as details on areas of your life you'd like to improve. Be as thorough as you like; the more context included in your request, the more personalized AI's response will be and the more thoughtful its subsequent questions for you to consider. In your first prompt, or when you're answering ChatGPT's questions, consider using the voice-to-text feature to provide faster and more natural reflections.

Sample Starter Prompt

I need you to play the role of an expert life coach with 20+ years of experience helping people discover their life's purpose and develop into the best version of themselves. Lately, I've been feeling overwhelmed and bogged down by my work and social commitments, while I've also started to neglect my health, passions, and hobbies. I want to become a better, more fulfilled version of the self I have been lately, with your help to guide me there.

Simulate a Coaching Session

Not a fan of ChatGPT's lengthier responses? Adjust your prompt to request a more conversational approach to your exploration, which will condense ChatGPT's responses and give you less to answer with each subsequent reply. Continue this back-and-forth for as long as you'd like. The more reflecting you do as a result of thoughtful questioning from ChatGPT, the more epiphanies about your life's goals and motivations you may have.

> Let's make this more conversational by pretending this is a coaching session, with me as your client. Keeping in mind all that we've already covered, you may begin.

Create an Action Plan

Once you feel that ChatGPT has a deep amount of context into your background, goals, skill sets, and motivations, you can prompt it to help you create a practical guide of personal development tactics and methods catered specifically to how you work, how you think, and what motivates you.

> Based on what you know about me and my motivations, please create a practical guide of different personal development tactics and methods that you might recommend as I pursue my growth. Be as detailed as possible on what the methods are and how to do them. Explain why you think each path would be useful to me, and feel free to ask me any additional questions you may have to help you refine these recommendations.

ACHIEVE GOALS

How AI Can Help You Set and Reach Your Goals

Knowing what you'd like to achieve or deciding what habit you'd like to change is often easy. But actually achieving that new goal or committing to a new habit is much harder. Just ask the vast majority of Americans who don't stick to their New Year's resolutions or reach their goals. ChatGPT can help you come up with a framework to set clearer, more specific goals, and then formulate a reasonable plan to help you achieve them.

Set Up Your Initial Request

If you generally understand what you want to achieve, ChatGPT can alter a vague resolution or lofty ideal into an actionable, achievable goal. In your prompt, share what you'd generally like to achieve, like eating healthier, running a 5K, or reading more. Provide context about what is motivating this goal, what your current state is relative to the goal, or if there are any hindrances you expect toward hitting the goal. By enlisting ChatGPT to help you organize your goal in the SMART (specific, measurable, achievable, relevant, time-bound) framework, you can establish a strong baseline to get very clear on your plan of action.

Sample Starter Prompt

My New Year's resolution is to read more and cut down on screen time. I currently start and stop books but rarely finish them, and I spend hours every day scrolling through social media. I genuinely enjoy reading but have fallen out of the habit. Also, I tend to "go big" with my resolutions and fall off the bandwagon quickly when I "mess up." I need your help setting a SMART (specific, measurable, achievable, relevant, time-bound) goal to achieve this habit. Then you may ask up to 5 questions to refine this SMART goal further.

Create a Timeline with Check-In Points

ChatGPT can help you create a plan toward achieving your goal with specific check-in points and provide measurement ideas that make sense for your goal. Consider your own preferences in your prompt—do you work best with frequent check-ins, or do you need a longer stretch to make progress? Are you more of a "rip off the Band-Aid and start" type person when it comes to new goals and habits, or are you better served by a gradual buildup to a bigger effort?

For my goal of reading more, I'd like your help in breaking down a clear 60-day plan with milestones and checkpoints to keep me motivated. Please also provide me with any tips you have on staying committed to my new goal/habit when it becomes harder. If all goes well, I should have read 2 books of ~350 pages by the end of 60 days. In your plan, please break down the process using the method of continual improvement through small, manageable steps.

Get Support from an Accountability Partner

Starting a new habit or working toward a difficult goal can be a lot easier if you are held accountable and are motivated and encouraged. AI can serve as an accountability partner, giving you a place to share reflections on your progress, get advice for roadblocks, or seek some encouragement. Requesting future interactions to be in conversational format ensures that ChatGPT will end its responses with a question to keep the conversation going, just as a coach or friend might. Once you've sent off this prompt, save the link to this particular chat and return to it whenever you need a little help from your new accountability buddy.

Acting as an accountability partner, I would like you to provide me with support, guidance, and motivation whenever I return to this chat to update you or provide reflections on my progress. Treat such answers as a conversation.

Stay Motivated Through Setbacks

No matter how tight your plan is or how important your goal, staying motivated to achieve or maintain your habits can be incredibly difficult. Distractions in your life can make your goals seem less important, a tendency toward perfectionism could hinder your ambition, and staying the course can be tough if you aren't seeing results or rewards from your progress just yet. In addition to being a motivational support that you can vent your struggles and frustrations to, ChatGPT can also provide you with helpful tips to persevere and get your motivation back.

> I've been feeling deeply unmotivated to hit my goal lately. Could you create a guide to getting my motivation back, complete with proven methods and little-known tips for getting back on the bandwagon?

AID DECISION-MAKING

How AI Can Help You Make Tough Decisions

When faced with a tough decision, it is often helpful to seek consultation from someone in your life with more subject matter experience to help you evaluate what decision may be best for you. But for many tough decisions, you may not necessarily have a trusted person in your network to discuss them with, or perhaps the decision is deeply personal and you are concerned others will judge or not listen objectively. ChatGPT can fill this gap. By articulating the details of the difficult decision you are trying to make, ChatGPT can offer perspective from a variety of roles.

Set Up Your Initial Request

In your first prompt, treat ChatGPT as you might a trusted friend. Type or speak all of the details of the decision you are struggling with, including as much context as possible. What are your initial feelings toward each path? What forces are pushing you one way or another? Why is this decision in particular so difficult for you? What background information is relevant? All of these are valid details to include in your initial prompt.

Sample Starter Prompt

> I am struggling to make a decision. <Add as much detail as possible for the decision, and describe what you have already thought through or are concerned about.> Acting as a trusted mentor with experience on matters like this, please thoughtfully summarize my dilemma in a pros and cons list for each of the potential decisions I could make based on the details I have given you.

Additional Ways to Personalize

Factor In Other Considerations

Now that you have a nicely organized pros and cons list, AI can help you think outside the box of the current what-if's that may be giving you tunnel vision in this decision-making process. Or it might be able to squeeze out a little extra clarity in that pros and cons list it has started for you. By answering the questions AI prompts you with for additional details, you can help the tool provide you with enhanced guidance through your decision-making process.

> I'm sure there are other things I should consider factoring into my decision that I have not yet accounted for in what I have shared with you. As an objective observer with this area of expertise, please share 10 other factors I should think about for my decision-making process. Please explain your reasoning and accompany each factor with a question for me to answer.

Learn What Other Research May Need to Be Done

Even if it feels like you've already done all the necessary research for your decision, there may still be a key element you haven't considered. Asking ChatGPT to suggest what other information you should seek before making a final decision will uncover something you might have missed. If any of the additional information you need could be found with some desktop research, bonus: AI can help you find that info fast!

> What additional information might I consider seeking out when making this decision?

Help Detect Where You May Already Be Leaning

You know how a friend offering an empathetic ear can sometimes tell where your mind is going before you yourself know for sure? ChatGPT is particularly skilled at this as well, detecting patterns in the language you use. Now that you've loaded it up with context, ask the tool to suggest where it thinks you might already be leaning and why, along with an updated pros and cons list.

> Now that you know more about the situation, please update my pros and cons list. Then conclude with a suggestion on which decision you think I might be leaning toward based on my answers to you, and explain why you think I may be leaning in this direction.

Find a Creative Solution

Not all decisions are black-and-white. If you feel backed into a corner with a particularly tough decision, you may feel like there is no possible in-between state, when in fact, there are likely many! ChatGPT can generate feasible scenarios where "both" options are pursuable, all while outlining the risks and benefits of each path. In doing so, you may find a path to get the best of both worlds.

> Are there any creative ways I could successfully pursue both options, without really having to make a firm decision at all? And if I do, what are the potential implications, risks, and benefits of pursuing alternate paths?

LEARN NEW SKILLS

How AI Can Help You Gain New Skills

If you have a new skill in mind that you want to learn but don't have any idea where to begin or what resources to leverage in your learning process, ChatGPT can guide you through what you need to learn, and the order in which to learn it, by creating a course outline for the skill of your choosing. Your AI tool will then generate details on the courses, providing you with plenty of material for you to ask even more questions about!

Set Up Your Initial Request

In your prompt, share what you would like to learn and where you are in your learning journey. Are you a total beginner? Are you picking a skill back up after many years away? Maybe you are already starting out fairly qualified but want to dig deeper. If you want to stick to the basics at first, you may suggest creating a "<Subject> for Beginners" course. Want to look ahead into more advanced topics? By adjusting your prompt to "<Subject>: From Beginner to Expert," you'll notice more advanced subject matter later in your course outline.

Sample Starter Prompt

I want to create a small vegetable garden, but I don't know where to start. Can you help me put together a "Gardening for Beginners" course? I'm interested in starting a small vegetable garden. The course should consist of modules and sub-lessons to cover everything I need to know as a beginner about how to prepare and grow a garden, choose plants, handle pests, and other important lessons.

Teach a Course, Step-by-Step

Next up, you should ask ChatGPT to write out a lesson for each section. This will give you a quick overview of the basics and prepare you to dive deeper into the other "recommended course materials." This approach helps you learn at your own pace while maintaining a clear path to proficiency in your new skill. Each new lesson will likely be a concise overview, and with each layer of subsequent prompting, you can go more in-depth and ask follow-up questions to get quick answers along the way.

> Please write out the contents for your proposed course "Module 2, Lesson 3: Planting Techniques" with robust details that a beginner should know about how to understand and execute each stage of this process.

Recommend Books on Your Topic of Interest

Want to dive deeper into a new subject but don't know where to begin? Instead of aimlessly wandering through the bookstore or scrolling an endless list of search results online, ChatGPT can help you rapidly come up with a list of books on the subject matter with details on the author's credentials, the book's ratings from readers, and a brief description of why the book may be worth reading for your particular interest. Prompts like this will also work for suggested YouTube channels, blogs, podcasts, and more.

> I am interested in learning more about lesser-known American history and about the people and groups that aren't often taught about in typical high school American history courses. I'm particularly interested in the periods between the end of the Civil War and the beginning of World War II. Please make a table of 10 recommended books where the columns are "Title and Author," "About the Author/Author's Credentials," "Description of the Book," and "Why It Might Appeal to Me."

Check Your Understanding

Explaining any subject back to your educator can help new learnings stick, in addition to helping you make sure you understand the subject matter. If you ever find that you are not 100% sure whether you understand a topic, simply write your explanation into ChatGPT and ask for feedback on the accuracy of your statement.

"<Articulate your understanding of the subject matter.>" In the statement in quotations, I've explained my understanding of <subject matter>. Is my understanding accurate, or is there anything flawed in my interpretation? Please provide critique or feedback so that I might learn.

SUMMARIZE LEARNING MATERIALS

How AI Can Help You Summarize Articles, Documents, and Videos

If you are an avid learner, there is no limit to the amount of educational information you can discover online to grow your knowledge. News articles, industry reports, YouTube videos...there's simply not enough time in the day to consume it all! Well, there's not enough time if you don't use AI. Just as generative AI tools can teach new concepts, they can also be skilled summarizers when given particular resources to reference. With these capabilities, you can leverage AI to skim and summarize materials, ask questions about them, and help you determine if it's worth investing even more time diving in deeper. Never upload copyrighted material, and check with your workplace's AI policy before uploading company documents.

Set Up Your Initial Request

If you have a lengthy document to read, like a PDF or a word document, you can upload it into an AI tool that allows for document attachments like Claude or ChatGPT. Once the document is uploaded, you can ask the AI tool as many questions as you'd like about its text content, whether to summarize the entire document or seek specific answers about what the document says. Have a spreadsheet? You can even upload these into ChatGPT and ask it questions about the data within, including asking it to spot any interesting trends or even create a graph visualizing the contents within!

Sample Starter Prompt

I have attached a PDF of a recent report I need to study for work. Could you summarize the key sections and takeaways within it and specifically share what it says about <topic> and in what section and on what page this occurs?

Additional Ways to Personalize

Summarize News Articles

Furthermore, with tools that allow for web browsing, you can often simply drop in the URL of the article and ask the tool to summarize it directly. Just know this will not work if the article is behind a paywall or if there are other similar restrictions to allowing access to AI tools. (For example, a number of publications are increasingly adding to their website code snippets that prevent crawling from AI tools.) For this reason, it is best to skim the beginning of articles to check how a summary compares to the actual contents.

Please summarize the key takeaways from this article <paste in link>.

Summarize Lectures on YouTube

If there is a lengthy TED Talk, uploaded college lecture, or educational webinar recording you want to watch but can't seem to find the time, Google's Gemini can be leveraged to summarize the key points in a video and help you determine if it's worth the full watch. You can even get it to provide you with a full transcription or ask at what point in the video a certain topic is discussed so you can skip ahead to what is most important to you. The only prerequisite to use Gemini in this way is to have the video be made publicly available on YouTube!

> Provide a detailed bullet-pointed summary of this video lecture as if you were a straight-A student attending the lecture and taking notes. Include all key points with clear explanations and helpful examples the professor provides, and highlight and define any key terms or vocabulary from the lecture <paste in video URL>.

LEARN A FOREIGN LANGUAGE

How AI Can Help You Practice Another Language

If you are learning a relatively common language like French or Spanish, ChatGPT can be an excellent aid in your learning process by acting as a tutor for whatever level of this new language you have achieved. It can be particularly effective in understanding language constructs and grammatical rules as well as reading, writing, and interpretation. Even if you are just beginning, you can ask ChatGPT to behave like your tutor in this language, creating a structured plan to teach you valuable lessons in the new language.

Set Up Your Initial Request

In your first prompt, provide ChatGPT with context on your current level of understanding of the language. You may also request your lesson to be conducted primarily in your first language (best for beginners), or you may be comfortable with the lessons being conducted in the language you are learning.

I would like you to act as a tutor of beginner-level French. I am very new to learning the language, so I will need you to tutor me primarily in the English language. I want to gradually get better at speaking and writing French while ensuring I understand the fundamentals. Please conduct my first lesson and be as thorough as possible. Include content for your first lesson; suggested homework; and, at the end, explain what our next lesson will be.

Additional Ways to Personalize ○

Execute Your Language-Learning Course

The starter prompt will generate something akin to a first class of a new language, including common phrases, suggested ways to practice, and homework to do on your own time. From there, you can continue to return to your chat by asking for "the next lesson." The beauty of AI tools like ChatGPT is you can control the pace and the subject matter, all through your prompts. If you'd like to change things up a bit or focus on a new area of language learning for your next lesson, just request that in your prompt!

In this next lesson, I'd like to learn about idiomatic phrases and common regional expressions.

Understand Grammar Rules for Foreign Languages

If you are struggling to understand, say, the nuances of verb conjugations for a new language, ChatGPT can create practical guides and explain grammar rules in easy-to-understand ways. Whether prompting it to explain when you might use a particular tense or asking for an in-depth breakdown of how to conjugate for all subjects of a specific verb, AI will help you on your way to proficiency quickly.

I'm having trouble understanding when to use the subjunctive verb tense in Italian, particularly when to use it over the indicative. Please explain the key situations where the subjunctive mood is used and provide a simple guide to conjugating *-are* verbs in the present subjunctive tense. Additionally, create a table breaking down how to conjugate such verbs in your response.

Expand Your Vocabulary

While you could always ask ChatGPT for a list of translated words common in a particular subject matter or topic, one of the most effective ways to expand your vocabulary is the understanding of words in context. ChatGPT can generate new texts for you to read in an instant, highlight the key vocabulary words, and even translate the text into English so that you can read and understand the full context.

I'm hoping to expand my understanding of the French vocabulary so I can use it when dining at a restaurant in France. Please generate a scripted conversation, entirely in French, that incorporates as many vocabulary words as possible for this scenario. Be sure to bold all keywords. After creating this conversation, please provide the translation with the same formatting in English.

Practice Reading Comprehension

AI can be a great aid in honing your reading comprehension skills in a foreign language. Start by either finding, copying, and pasting an excerpt of text written in the language into the prompt field, or attach a PDF containing writing in the other language. Alternatively, you could even ask ChatGPT to generate a piece of writing in the other language for you, as in the following prompt. From there, ask ChatGPT to quiz you on the writing sample or article by asking you questions for you to answer in your first language. Or, for an extra challenge, answer in the language you are learning!

I am trying to improve my reading comprehension of the French language. Please write a random article about any topic that has vocabulary words that someone with an intermediate French language understanding might know. After you have written the article, I will read it then. When I tell you to "quiz me," I would like you to ask me questions (in English) about what you wrote to test my reading comprehension.

Practice Conversing in Another Language

You can use ChatGPT's voice feature, accessible by tapping the "headphones" icon in the official app, to practice conversing in the foreign language you are learning. You can choose a couple of approaches for this kind of practice: You can prompt ChatGPT for a simple back-and-forth conversation (recommended for when you are more advanced in the language), or you can ask for more feedback as you converse.

Not only can ChatGPT speak the language back to you; it can also provide a critique on your word choice or grammar. In the former scenario, ChatGPT might behave more like a local speaker, aiming to understand you despite your grammatical errors while continuing the conversation. In the latter scenario, ChatGPT will behave more as a tutor, from which you can choose to receive critiques in the language you are speaking or in your first language.

One last tip here—when you leverage this use case for ChatGPT, the app is generally good at nailing pronunciation in these common languages, especially if it is one of the thirty-plus languages available within your app's "speech" settings. Generally, this is set to "auto-detect" the language being spoken and respond accordingly. However, if you are starting your initial prompt in English and the pronunciation of the non-English response doesn't sound accurate (or if ChatGPT is responding too much in English), adjusting your "speech" settings temporarily to the language you want to speak can be helpful.

> I am hoping to improve my French speaking skills. Please have a conversation back and forth with me in the French language, using common words found in beginner-level French classes. The scenario is 2 friends talking about their past weekend. If I mispronounce something or say something incorrectly, you should stop the conversation for a moment and correct me. Tell me what I said wrong, what I probably meant to say or should have said, and then continue the conversation where we left off.

STUDY AND PREPARE FOR TESTS

How AI Can Help You with Academic Prep

If you are a student preparing for an upcoming exam, AI tools can function as a study partner who actually stays on task. For this use case, it is helpful to have typed class notes to upload into the tools with attachment capabilities like ChatGPT or Claude. Don't have typed notes? Even an upload of your class syllabus with details on what sections you are preparing for can be helpful. The AI tool can create questions to quiz you on and provide feedback on your answers.

Set Up Your Initial Request

In your prompt, provide as much detail as possible on the subject matter of your upcoming test and what kind of study help you seek. Uploaded attachments can do a lot of the heavy lifting for providing context. Then get specific on what you'd like help with. For example, do you need help understanding a certain topic, or would you like some practice questions to answer and receive feedback on?

If you don't have typed notes, this study help can still work for broader popular subjects like history or undergraduate sciences, for which there is a wealth of information that AI tools have been trained upon. For more obscure subjects, though, it is best to use your notes, or at least have them and your reading materials handy to compare against.

Sample Starter Prompt

I am studying for the AP US History Exam, and I would like your help as my study buddy. I have attached my notes from my history class this year for reference, but I recognize they may not be thorough enough. I would like you to ask me, one by one, questions I can answer to best prepare me for my test, based on my notes or your understanding of the AP US History Exam. I would like all of the questions to be short-answer style.

You should ask me one question at a time, then wait for me to answer. After I have answered, you can reveal the correct answer and explain whether I am right or wrong, and why if necessary. Then you can ask me the next question.

Additional Ways to Personalize

Improve Your Test-Taking Skills

No one is born a natural at taking tests. Oftentimes, your ability to perform well on school exams and standardized tests depends upon how much training you've had on understanding the test's structure, how it's graded, or how to approach different types of exam sections, from multiple choice to reading comprehension to essay writing. If you never received that kind of guidance, taking tests, especially standardized ones, can be a lot more difficult. The good news is: ChatGPT can help bridge that knowledge gap and share strategies to improve your test-taking abilities!

> Multiple-choice questions have always tripped me up on tests. Create a guide for how to critically analyze answer choices to determine the most likely correct answer. Please also detail common tricks used when writing multiple-choice questions, as well as common mistakes students often make when answering them.

Overcome Test Anxiety

Many students struggle with test anxiety, especially high performers with a tendency toward perfectionism. ChatGPT can offer guidance for handling test anxiety, with suggestions for how to prepare ahead of the examination and handle stress during the actual test. In this prompt, detail specifics on any triggers that you've noticed cause you extra stress during a test, like time management concerns, second-guessing yourself on the multiple choice section, and so on. Explaining your past experiences can be helpful for more personalized guidance.

I experience significant test anxiety before and during standardized tests, and I have one coming up. In the past, multiple-choice tests in particular have really tripped me up, and I spend so much time second-guessing myself that I often have trouble finishing. I need your help creating a comprehensive guide to decrease this anxiety before the test, as well as specific strategies to ground myself and focus on the task at hand. I need both mental preparation techniques and even psychological or physical tricks that can help.

MAKE A PRIORITIZED TO-DO LIST

If you are ever feeling overwhelmed with the many things on your plate, AI can help you rapidly sort through the mental chaos and craft a thoughtful to-do list—then share recommendations on the order in which to prioritize your tasks. Start by tapping the microphone to speak out loud everything on your mind, venting all the things you have to get done and any context that would be useful for prioritization. Does anything have a deadline, for example, or how long might the task reasonably take? From there, use the following prompt for a nicely summarized take on your to-dos. You can then use ChatGPT to track what's been done or not by returning to the chat with details on what has been accomplished, then seek guidance on how to efficiently tackle the rest of the items.

<List out the many things you have to do with as much context as possible.> I need your help taking my ramblings and turning them into a to-do list capturing everything that needs to get done. I would like you to list these to-dos in an order that will account for both priority as well as efficiently reducing the tasks on my list as fast as possible. Using the context I've provided, please estimate the time I should allot to complete each task and explain your reasoning for the order you have provided.

ANSWER RANDOM CURIOSITIES IN-DEPTH

One of the best and most frequent ways I use AI is to address the random curiosities that pop into my head throughout the day. Whereas previously I might have turned to an Internet search engine to find answers, it can take a while to sift through the results, and then from there you must click through and read a potentially very lengthy article to find the answers you seek. By contrast, ChatGPT and tools like it offer a nice in-depth summary to answer your queries, not only offering you the answer to your original question but often expanding on the topic a little further to provide even more context and explanation. As an important reminder though, if you are using AI in this way to help end a heated debate or make a strong point, you should seek a secondary source if the stakes are high, just to be sure none of the information was hallucinated.

I just finished watching the film *Marie Antoinette*, directed by Sofia Coppola. Could you summarize for me which elements of the film's story were historically accurate and which were not, calling out some of the biggest differences?

SIMPLIFY COMPLEX TOPICS

When you are exploring a complex topic (or faced with an overly complex response), a simple adjustment to your prompt can make things a lot more digestible. Adding "Explain it to me like I'm 12" to the end of your query is the simplest way to accomplish this. However, depending on the kind of explanation you are looking for, this could end in an oversimplification. A slightly lengthier prompt can guide you to an explanation that is free from jargon and explained well enough for a novice on the subject to understand.

I want to understand more about the primary theories around quantum physics. Please explain these in a way that someone completely new to the topic would understand, without using technical language or jargon. I'm looking for an explanation that breaks down these complex ideas into simple concepts, while still getting at the core theory.

HELP OVERCOME PROCRASTINATION

Most of us suffer from occasional bouts of procrastination. ChatGPT can offer guidance on how to overcome this challenge, perhaps by suggesting new ideas you haven't tried yet, helping you reframe your mindset, or recommending specific types of motivational support. Be as honest as possible about what you are feeling, what you are trying to avoid, and what might be causing that avoidance. ChatGPT will help you come up with actionable ways to move forward.

I have been procrastinating big-time on starting my fitness routine. Even though every night I promise myself I'll start at the gym in the morning, when morning comes I always find an excuse—I didn't sleep well enough, it's too cold outside, I can't find the workout clothes I like, and so on. Can you help me identify why I just can't seem to get started? How can I reframe my mindset and just get started?

HELP CHILDREN WITH SCHOOL SUBJECTS

When children are struggling in a subject at school, it's not unusual for them to turn to their parents for help and guidance. After all, it can be difficult to remember the ins and outs of long division or exactly how a bill becomes a law. When faced with this challenge, tools like ChatGPT can help you help your child take on the academic challenges they are facing.

> My 11-year-old son is learning about photosynthesis in his science class. I barely remember or understand the science behind the topic myself! I need you to (1) explain the process of photosynthesis clearly to me, (2) provide me with a relatable analogy or metaphor that I can explain to my 11-year-old, and (3) suggest an activity we might do at home to help make the lesson stick.

PROVIDE PROMPTS TO INSPIRE YOU

Have you thought about journaling but aren't sure what to write about? Or maybe you need a little inspiration for a painting subject or other artistic habit you are trying to cultivate. With a simple prompt, you can leverage AI to provide you with a list of prompts to inspire your next endeavor. Detail what kinds of prompts you are looking for and what details would be most helpful for your use case.

> I am challenging myself to try to spend 30 minutes a day practicing my creative writing habits. I'm interested in trying fiction, fantasy, or sci-fi writing (with stories about humans but in nonfiction scenarios). Please provide me with 10 specific, distinct, and interesting writing prompts to inspire the start of each mini-writing session. These should be a premise for a small scene, suggesting a premise, character, and setting.

CHAPTER 8

Relationships and Social Skills

In our increasingly digital world, we can simultaneously be more connected with each other while also feeling further apart. Most of us have more interactions, but a smaller proportion of them are face-to-face. Your circle of acquaintances and friends might be large, but keeping up with so many people may make it more difficult to hone your focus on the relationships that are most important to you.

AI can help you become a better partner, family member, and friend, in spite of the chaos and demands of modern life! In this chapter, we'll dive into the many ways you can leverage AI to connect and communicate more effectively so that you can strengthen bonds with friends and loved ones in your life.

Whether you are looking to nurture more romance with your partner, resolve conflict with a coworker, set clear boundaries, or plan incredible get-togethers, there are unlimited ways to embrace AI as a resource in building stronger and healthier relationships.

STRENGTHEN RELATIONSHIPS

How AI Can Help You Build Strong Relationships

In a popular TED Talk, professor of psychiatry at Harvard Medical School Robert Waldinger revealed: "The people who were most satisfied with their relationships at age 50 were the healthiest at age 80." This conclusion came from an eighty-year-long Harvard study that Waldinger helped direct. Indeed, building stronger, healthier relationships with your loved ones is a fantastic way to bolster your health. And no matter where you are in your relationships, AI can serve as a helpful guide and inspirational support, introducing you to proven relationship-strengthening methods and easy-to-implement suggestions.

Set Up Your Initial Request

ChatGPT can provide personalized recommendations for the relationships in your life you most want to nurture. Start by sharing your relationship goals with ChatGPT and detail any obstacles that may be getting in the way of your goals. To drive more personalization, request that ChatGPT ask *you* questions to answer about your relationships.

Sample Starter Prompt

I want to improve my relationships with the people in my life who matter the most to me. These include my wife, teenage son, 10-year-old daughter, parents, sibling who lives in another state with her family, and good friends from high school, some of whom live nearby and some far. <Optional: Provide details on challenges you may be facing.> Help me craft a plan to reinvigorate my relationships so that I can better prioritize my time and life around them. Then ask me 10 questions to help you better refine a personalized plan for me.

Dive Further Into Each Relationship in Your Plan

Once you've responded to the questions asked of you (hint: use the voice-to-text transcription feature to save some time!), the AI tool will adapt its plan to provide even more personalized advice. From there, continue the conversation! To keep this reflection and guide in-depth, you may want to start focusing on a plan for one person at a time or get more specific recommendations.

> Let's make a more focused plan for my teenage son. He's very busy with extracurriculars (soccer) and school, and that combined with my work schedule makes quality time on weekdays hard. Could you recommend 10 father-son bonding activities that won't seem "lame" to a teen?

Plan Great Dates with Your Partner

Hoping to rekindle romance with your partner? ChatGPT can come up with a wide variety of memorable date ideas in moments. You can start with a general list of recommendations or get very detailed from the start. What should the vibe be—romantic, adventurous, laid-back? What kinds of things do you and your partner like or dislike? Do you want a fun and unique activity at home, or would you like to go out to a nearby spot?

> Recommend 10 distinct date night ideas for a Friday evening/night in May in Austin, TX, that a married couple might enjoy on a night out away from their kids. Provide a mix of fun, romantic, and free ideas.

Set Strong Boundaries

For the people-pleasers among us, saying no or "not right now" to friendly acquaintances, coworkers, or social groups can be tough, even if your time is genuinely limited. Setting boundaries with family members can be even harder. With ChatGPT's help, you can get detailed guidance on how to strengthen the quality of your relationships through building stronger boundaries with those who may demand more than you can give.

My parents regularly stop by unannounced and stay a long while, which often causes disruption to our family's schedule and eats into the little family time my partner and I get with my children. While I still want to see my parents, the frequency of their visits is harming more than helping our relationship. Create a robust guide to effectively establish firmer boundaries with them, including tips on what to do if these boundaries are ignored.

Connect over Long Distances

When those you love are farther away, maintaining a sense of closeness can be more difficult. ChatGPT can empower you to connect with these friends in more ways than just the occasional phone call or text, providing creative ideas to create memories together even at a distance. Ask for a list of general ideas, or get specific, detailing some of your shared interests to consider when planning a virtual hang.

My 3 best friends from college and I all live in different states. I want to create more memories with them even when we are far apart. Could you recommend 10 unique and distinct ways we might accomplish this?

ENGAGE BETTER WITH OTHERS

How AI Can Help You Thoughtfully
Engage with Others

People are made up of so many layers that often inform their identity and sense of self, from where they are from, to the student groups they were a part of in high school, to even what Hogwarts House they say they belong to. Whether or not you believe in the efficacy of things like home state, astrology signs, or personality tests for adequately describing a person and their motivation and behavior, many people do. So when a coworker, a friend, or a relative chooses to share whatever identifier they have assigned themselves, you should consider this a great gift because they have just given you insight to better understand and communicate with them.

Set Up Your Initial Request

There can be any number of reasons why you want to better understand the identifier this person has shared with you, like their Myers-Briggs personality type or astrological sign. He could be a coworker you're having trouble working with. She could be a new friend going through a tough time. Whatever the reason, if you don't feel comfortable directly getting insights from this person, ChatGPT can act as a guiding light. Start by sharing with ChatGPT a little about your situation, this person's relationship to you, and what they've shared about themselves, and request a guide to this personality type.

Sample Starter Prompt

My new boss says she's an ISTJ. Create a guide to what that means about her personality type, especially when it comes to her approach to work or management.

Additional Ways to Personalize

Compare Against Your Own Personality Type

After you've gotten a good overview of this personality type, in your next prompt you can get more specific about your situation and what you are hoping to accomplish. Are you hoping to get ahead of miscommunications? Are you hoping to motivate someone? Are you trying to get this person to open up? If you know your personality type, you can even ask ChatGPT to unpack your type and highlight key similarities and differences. You can ask it to "compare" personalities across different typing structures—try crossing a Myers-Brigg type with an astrological sign, or a DiSC assessment with an Enneagram.

I want to get off on the right foot with my ISTJ boss. Is there anything I should consider doing or avoiding? I am an ENFP and an "I" DiSC type, if that helps.

Improve Your Cultural Competence

Whether you are traveling to another country for business or you have met a new neighbor with a cultural background different from your own, ChatGPT can help you learn more about how to thoughtfully engage, increasing your understanding of common differences in communication styles across cultures.

I am preparing for a business trip to Japan. I want to be sure to follow proper business etiquette that's aligned with Japanese business customs while there. What should I consider when engaging with these potential business partners? What are common mistakes an American businessperson might make that I should avoid?

Foster Inclusivity

Whether at work, at school, or online, you probably interact daily with people from a variety of cultures and backgrounds. Especially for professional environments, ChatGPT can educate you on appropriate communication practices and help you become more aware of sayings or phrases that might exclude or devalue others in your circle.

I lead a diverse team of young professionals and have gotten feedback that my turns of phrase might be a bit outdated. I want to improve my awareness of language sensitivities, particularly in the work environment, so that my team feels safe and included. Please start by giving me 20 commonly used terms or actions in a business environment that might cause discomfort, explain the reason for this sensitivity, and propose an alternative more respectful phrase or action.

RESOLVE CONFLICTS

How AI Can Help You with Conflict Resolution

Most of us don't like conflict. But most of us also don't like backing down from conflict when challenged. If you are conflict-avoidant or if there's a handful of people in your life you regularly find yourself bickering with, turn to ChatGPT to help guide you toward a grounded and empathetic approach to conflict resolution.

AI's advice can be useful for preparing for inevitable tough conversations, but it can particularly be helpful for handling text-based conflicts. Those have unfortunately become more frequent, whether in social media, text messages, or workplace communications.

Set Up Your Initial Request

While you might feel like saying *exactly* what is on your mind in the middle of a conflict, in the future, it could be read by others (or yourself) in a negative light. So before you send that message, detail to ChatGPT the specific scenario you are dealing with, the tone you want to strike in your message (and perhaps what tone you'd like to avoid), and give it your potential message. Ask it to, as an objective observer, evaluate your tone and tell you where you might be missing the mark, and ask for suggestions on what you might adjust.

Sample Starter Prompt

My boss is nagging me in a public Slack channel about a report that I haven't had time to finish—because I've had 10 other "hot" items thrown on my plate since it was assigned. I need to respond and want to come off as firm, calm, and professional, not defensive or annoyed (even though I am very annoyed). Below is the message I've drafted. Could you evaluate the tone and tell me where I can improve? <Paste your message.>

Rewrite or Rephrase Your Initial Message

Sometimes, you might just be too livid to even attempt to draft a professional or at least well-intentioned message. The last thing on your mind may be protecting the feelings of those who have wronged you. This is a situation in which ChatGPT can be particularly helpful. Instead of telling James *exactly where* he can find that report or ripping Tricia a new one, turn to ChatGPT. Share your situation and "vent" to ChatGPT with all the deep frustrations you have, then ask it to propose three ways to communicate your issues and needs in a palatable and professional tone.

> My coworker has asked me for the exact same document 10 times now. Every time they ask me to drop everything, find the document, and send it to them again. I'm so frustrated! I'd like to tell them that they are wasting my time and it's shocking they haven't figured out how to find it themselves by now. But I want to do my best to stay professional and even-keeled. Please give me 3 suggestions for what to say to them to get my feedback across while still sounding professional and maintaining our working relationship. Make it concise and appropriate for a Microsoft Teams message. <Paste your message.>

Consider Their Perspective

Asking the other person to share their deeper motivations or feelings around their stance is an obvious course of action for better conflict resolution—but it's very difficult to do in the moment. In this situation, you can turn to ChatGPT to provide possible reasons for what this other person has done or said. Ask ChatGPT to simulate their point of view and articulate underlying beliefs and motivations. By putting ChatGPT "in their shoes," you may be able to get a little closer to the issue or at least ground yourself in a place of assuming positive intent for this other person and help ease your own frustration.

My partner and I recently got into a heated argument about <topic>. We left the conversation both feeling hurt and upset. I wanted <your wants>, and they wanted <their wants>. <Add in additional detail about the conflict.> So that I can reapproach my partner with more empathy on this issue, could you help me try to better understand what their perspective might be and what could be driving their feelings and behavior on this issue? Give me 5 possible reasons.

Get Advice for Addressing the Issue

After you have provided sufficient context on the conflict you have been dealing with, ChatGPT can give you clear, actionable advice on how to address the problem to hopefully result in a better outcome for both parties.

Give me advice for clear, specific, and actionable next steps for reopening this conversation and resolving this issue. Include the reasoning behind your advice.

Simulate a Tough Conversation

If you are nervous about an upcoming confrontation with this other person, ChatGPT's voice feature can help you role-play out loud how the scenario might play out. In your first prompt, detail the role you would like ChatGPT to play—including any characteristics of this person that might be helpful for the simulation. For example: Are they avoidant? Stubborn? Defensive? Do they lash out? What is their perspective on the issue at hand? How do you expect them to react to this situation? By practicing a little, you'll feel more confident and prepared for the conversations you may be dreading.

I need you to help me role-play an important discussion I need to have with my partner. It is about our family finances and how their tendency to buy extravagant items without discussing it with me is really harming our ability to save any money. When I've tried to address things in the past, they deflect, change the subject, or insist everything is fine as is. They can also get defensive. I need you to play the role of my partner and help me practice how to approach this conversation with them.

GIVE GREAT GIFTS

How AI Can Help You Give Great Gifts

If you haven't been blessed with the skill of incredible gift giving, or if you are usually good at gifting but you just have that one relative you can never find *anything* for, AI has you covered! Using a single tool with web-browsing capabilities, you can not only brainstorm personalized gift ideas, but you can also source items readily available to purchase online.

Set Up Your Initial Request

Start by sharing with ChatGPT as much detail as you can about your gifting situation and your gift receiver. What is the occasion for your gift? What is your ideal budget? Most importantly, share what you can about the gift receiver—their relationship to you, their hobbies and interests, and perhaps information about any successful gifts from the past.

Sample Starter Prompt

I need your help coming up with ideas for a birthday gift for my mother on her 70th birthday. She always claims she "has too much stuff" and "doesn't want anything," but I want to get her something special regardless. My budget is $150. Her interests include flower arranging and baking, and she's recently gotten into meditation and yoga. Please give me 10 ideas and provide the estimated price range for this type of gift.

Additional Ways to Personalize

Get Specific Product Recommendations

Once you've got your list of gift ideas, you can leverage AI tools with web-browsing functionality to search the web for more specific products, summarizing the offering, the price, and what customers say about it, while providing a link to a place where you can learn more and possibly make a purchase.

> I like the idea of a personalized yoga mat. Maybe something with a floral or nature-inspired print or something I can customize? Using your web-browsing feature, please provide me with recommendations for where I might purchase a high-quality yoga mat, and, in particular, point out where I might have something custom-made. For each recommendation, provide details on why people recommend this product or brand.

Get Inspiration for a Custom-Made Gift Basket

Sometimes a themed gift basket is just the thing to make someone's day, especially if it is built around a personal hobby or made to serve a particular purpose. Give ChatGPT the context around the situation, the maximum amount of money you'd like to spend, and any details on your recipient that might make it a little more special.

> I want to make a care package for a friend who just had her first baby, filled with products that would be very useful for a new mom (including some unexpected things not found in typical premade baskets!). Recommend 15 items to choose from and give an estimated price point for each. I'll likely end up choosing 6 or 7 and don't want to spend more than $75.

Get Ideas for Homemade Gifts

Whether you are on a budget, love giving truly unique gifts, or just enjoy getting creative for the holidays, homemade gifts can be a great solution. AI can help you come up with ideas for a perfect homemade gift on any budget. Start with a general request detailing the occasion and the recipients (family, classmates, coworkers, etc.) to get targeted ideas for the proposed gift.

> I'm on a tight budget and want to try my hand at making gifts for Christmas this year. I'm open to anything, so long as the gift can be crafted by a beginner and costs less than $15 per person when made in bulk. I want

to create gifts for 15 people, ranging in age from 15 to 85. I'd like to make the same thing for everyone but personalize them in some way or other. Give me 10 suggestions for what I could make.

Get Guidance on Creating Your Homemade Gift

Once you've got an idea of what could be made, ChatGPT can guide you through the step-by-step process of what making the items will look like and estimate the cost of supplies. If you are exploring multiple options, this is a great way to quickly get an understanding of the time, effort, and cost involved for each potential DIY idea! After you decide what to create, leverage an AI with web-browsing capability to find a tutorial video to help guide your process.

Make a detailed step-by-step guide for creating homemade candles for 15 people. Include a list of ingredients necessary to make 15 candles and estimate the cost of purchasing that amount for each ingredient.

DELIVER MEMORABLE SPEECHES

How AI Can Help You Deliver Memorable Speeches

You've been asked to give a speech at a special event to honor someone you love. You want to honor the request, but you have no idea how to write or deliver such a speech! Instead of pulling your hair out or spending hours caught up in writer's block, you can turn to your favorite AI chatbot for guidance and inspiration.

Set Up Your Initial Request

In your prompt, tell ChatGPT a little more about the situation. What kind of event is the speech for? What's your relationship to the person being honored? Have you been given a rough estimate of how long you should talk? Give it all that background, then request that it make a guide to best practices for such a speech. Thanks to ChatGPT's context memory, the guide it creates will serve as a prompt context for your speech's future development.

I have been asked to deliver a speech at my good friend's wedding, and I need your guidance on how to craft an excellent speech. Please create a detailed guide to the elements of a great wedding speech.

Additional Ways to Personalize ──●

Create a Sample Speech Template

Now that you have a detailed breakdown of what goes into crafting a great speech, you can leverage this information to guide your next output. To help overcome any mental blocks, ask ChatGPT to sample a templated draft of such a speech for you. It will produce a structured sample speech with fill-in-the-blanks and a suggested time breakdown that you can reference when crafting your speech!

Please make a sample template to follow for a speech like this. I need the speech to be about 5 minutes long.

Uncover Personalized Details

Now that you've got a strong sense of the structure, it's time to personalize your speech to that individual and the situation. Have ChatGPT ask you a series of questions to help inform and inspire the context of your speech. By using the voice-to-text feature, you can easily answer these questions out loud, as if you are being casually interviewed by ChatGPT. You don't need to answer all the questions. As you answer these questions, if you find yourself at a loss but have an idea of how you might want to say something, just include that in your answer. For example, "Well, they are big fans of the Lord of the Rings movies—if I can somehow tie in a quote or theme from those movies to answer this question, that would be great."

Ask me 15 questions I can answer to help personalize the context of this speech.

Create a Personalized Outline

At this point, you'll have enough information to craft the speech on your own. However, if you are still feeling stuck, ChatGPT can help you outline (or even fully draft) your speech, keeping in mind the structure previously established and incorporating those personalized details.

Keeping in mind the speech structure we have established and the answers to my questions, please create a personalized bulleted outline for my speech. You need not include all my answers—only those that will fit nicely in the speech structure!

Get Guidance for Delivery

Finally, as you prepare for the big event, ChatGPT can provide tips and tricks for practicing and delivering your speech. Start with a request for a guide, or speak more specifically about any elements you are struggling with to get even more detailed guidance.

Create a guide to how I might successfully and confidently deliver this speech, as well as any advice on what else I can do to make this speech especially memorable or unique.

THROW STELLAR PARTIES

How AI Can Help You Throw Cool Parties

Whether you are throwing a casual get-together or have volunteered to host a celebration for a special event in someone else's life, ChatGPT can help even the most entertaining-inept person host a memorable party. AI is especially good at planning parties with a certain niche theme. From getting you started with party ideas and clever invitations to special games, activities, menus, and more, you'll save hours of planning when you leverage AI.

Set Up Your Initial Request

Laying the groundwork for ChatGPT in your first prompt is always a good place to start. What kind of party are you throwing and for whom? How much time can you dedicate to planning the party? Are you throwing it at your home or elsewhere? What is your budget? Maybe you don't have many of these things figured out yet. That's perfectly fine. ChatGPT can help you fill in the gaps!

Sample Starter Prompt

I'm throwing my best friend and her husband a couple's baby shower in 2 months. She is expecting a baby girl. I'll be hosting the party at my home from 2:00 p.m. to 5:00 p.m., with about 40 guests (both men and women). I know I want the shower to have a "jungle" theme because that is the theme of her nursery. I've never hosted an event like this before. Please create a detailed guide breaking down key elements of great baby showers to draw inspiration from.

Additional Ways to Personalize

Create Unique Invitations

A unique invitation can add a little extra delight to your invitee's inbox and can be a memorable keepsake for your guests of honor. A great way to make the party invitation a little more personalized is to include a short themed poem that features details about the event. With ChatGPT, you can quickly generate multiple ideas for the poem and revise from there!

I now need your help crafting a short 8–10-line poem that will be used on the invitation to guests, thoughtfully incorporating phrases aligned with the theme. Please create 4 poem options for me to choose from.

Get Ideas for On-Theme Party Food and Drinks

Themed bites and drinks can make a party all the more special. ChatGPT can help you brainstorm ideas for what you can serve, create recipes for how to make them, and even come up with clever on-theme names for your menu items to display on your serving table.

> I'm trying to come up with a fun menu featuring savory and sweet treats, light bites, and beverages/mocktails that can be featured at this baby shower. Help me come up with 15 on-theme ideas. Include the theme name and a description of the ingredients.

Create a Party Playlist

If you want to incorporate some background tunes on the big day, filled with well-loved songs that also appropriately fit the theme and occasion of your party, ChatGPT can act as your party DJ. If you have a rough idea of the kind of music you'd like featured, include these as examples in your prompt for an even more personalized playlist.

> Help me come up with 40 song ideas for a party playlist to fit the theme and occasion. Feature songs that may be jungle-inspired, or with lyrics that have something to do with having a baby or a little girl. Two examples I'll be including are "You'll Be in My Heart" from the movie *Tarzan* and "Isn't She Lovely?" by Stevie Wonder. Help me come up with the rest and explain your suggestions.

Create a Unique and Personalized Party Game

Hoping to have some activities that guests can enjoy at the party? Get ideas and instructions instantly from ChatGPT and collaborate to come up with a new idea of your own! Start by asking ChatGPT to recommend unique party games or activities, specifying if you want these to be something the full group does together or more casual activities to enjoy as they mingle. If you have a budget for supplies or want to keep mess at a minimum, include requests like these in your prompt as well.

Help me come up with 10 low-cost ideas for unique activities that guests at the baby shower can participate in while milling about at the party. These should be fun and engaging, but not so involved that they cannot hold a conversation while they play. Guest participation should be kept to no more than 10 minutes. For each activity, please detail the materials required, if any.

Craft Unique Decorations with AI Art

A fun and efficient way to make your themed party even more exciting? Create custom AI art decorations! The incredible thing about using AI for this is you can instantly create images with uniquely customized elements that you may not be able to find anywhere else, combining elements of your themes with the interests of the honored guests, for example.

Use your prompt to describe the image, the art style you'd like it to use, or any kind of color palette you might like incorporated. Have fun with it! Once you've got an image you like, you can download it, enhance it in your AI's "photo enhancer" tool to boost the quality and size for larger prints, then have it printed. Bonus? It can be a fun souvenir for your honored guests (or, at the very least, a great conversation piece!).

Make an image of a baby elephant in a little pink tutu and bow dancing on a Broadway stage. The backdrop should show the stage's elegant proscenium, and the scenery in the backdrop should be a simple landscape of the jungle and blue sky above. The image should be in a watercolor style featuring soft pastels as the color palette throughout. Suitable for a baby shower.

NAVIGATE PARENTHOOD

How AI Can Help You Navigate Parenthood

Don't worry—I'm not going to tell you to let AI raise your children. *However*, AI can support you as you navigate the highs and lows of parenthood. From navigating questions about childhood development to confronting teenage behavior and different tactics to try, ChatGPT and other AI tools' vast training data gives you access to instant answers, as if you had a whole library of parenting books, articles, resources, and guides at the ready.

Set Up Your Initial Request

For parents, every year (or, for new parents, every month!) brings new exciting discoveries and new parenting challenges. As children learn and grow, their interests, behaviors, skills, and maturity levels change and fluctuate as well. Sparking a conversation with ChatGPT can provide you with insights into what you might expect or look out for in the year to come. Provide your child's age and your concerns or specific questions, or ask for a general guide. You can then ask follow-up questions on topics that are of particular interest to you as you prepare for parenting in this new phase of childhood.

Sample Starter Prompt

My infant is rapidly becoming a toddler, which is exciting (and a little scary, as her mobility now gives her free reign of the house!). Drawing from some of the most popular and well-regarded parenting books, create a detailed guide on what to expect from this new age and how to prepare.

Get Advice on Common Parenting Challenges

Whatever challenge you are facing, think of ChatGPT in this scenario as a helpful parent friend or a childhood behavior consultant who has seen it all. Detail the specifics of the parenting challenge or question you are dealing with, and be sure to include the age of the child to elicit age-appropriate advice. At the end of your initial prompt, you may also consider asking ChatGPT to ask *you* questions. By answering these questions, you'll subsequently receive even more specific tactics to consider.

> My 5-year-old is an incredibly picky eater and is unfortunately not fond of much outside of chicken nuggets and potato chips at the moment. She doesn't even want her foods to touch! She can't eat nuggets forever, but I also can't let her starve. Acting as a consultant in childhood behavior, create a detailed list of suggestions for how I might get her to try (and enjoy) new foods. Then ask me 10 questions that might help you better understand my predicament.

Answer All Those Questions

Kids—especially younger ones—are notorious for having a *lot* of questions. And they naturally expect their parents to have *all* the answers. Of course, parents understandably come up with lackluster answers sometimes, which inevitably will invite more questions. But what if you could easily nurture their curiosity and explain complex topics in a way they can learn and understand? With ChatGPT, you can do just that.

> My 7-year-old has been very fascinated with the weather lately—the clouds and their shapes in particular. I've been getting a lot of questions I don't quite know how to answer—why are they fluffy sometimes and sometimes flat? Where do they go? How does rain work? I want to be able to answer, but I honestly don't know myself. Please explain each answer to me so that I can better break it down for my child.

Help with Hard Conversations

Parents are the chief educators in children's lives, and thus they carry the burden of having a *lot* of difficult conversations. You might feel unprepared for some of the topics that arise, especially when the conversation comes about unexpectedly.

When faced with these situations—and you inevitably will encounter them as a parent—ChatGPT can serve as a support, giving you templates, guided talking points, general advice, and even tips for further reading to help you navigate any discomfort or nerves *you* feel about the situation. In your prompt, be sure to supply the age of your child, the conversation you need to have, and a rough understanding of any personal beliefs or perspectives you feel necessary to convey in your conversation.

I've recently learned that my daughter's fourth-grade class will be introduced to the concepts of puberty in class in a couple of months. I want to make sure the first time she learns about these things is from her mother, not her teachers or classmates. I want to introduce these concepts in ways that are not scary, inviting questions if she has them, while also covering all the things she'll likely be taught. Please help! I need a robust guide with specific suggestions and talking points to work from.

GET HELP WITH LETTERS OF RECOMMENDATION

A strong letter of recommendation can make a big difference in someone's life, especially people applying to college or those getting started with a new career or industry. While it's an honor to be asked to write one, these can take a lot of thought and time. But with ChatGPT, you can write a thoughtful, personalized, and well-structured letter quickly! Start by asking what elements make a strong letter of recommendation for this particular scenario. Then have it give you some questions to consider to inspire the content of your own letter. Have it draft a sample letter incorporating those personal details. Edit from there to ensure honesty and to adjust to your own voice.

> I have been asked to write a letter of recommendation for a college student who used to work after school at my restaurant as a waitress. She is now applying for a sales role at a tech company. Give me ideas for how I might write a letter that translates my experience in employing her as a waitress to why she'd be a good fit for this new role. Then write a templated example letter for me to use as inspiration.

GIVE BETTER FEEDBACK TO A PARTNER OR FRIEND

Feedback, when delivered well, can be a gift for both the receiver and the giver. The process can strengthen your relationship with the person, either in professional or personal situations (see Chapter 5 for advice on giving professional feedback). However, giving effective feedback is a bit of an art. ChatGPT can help you learn to structure your feedback in a way that is more likely to be well-received and listened to. Tell ChatGPT a little about the situation, what feedback you are trying to give and to whom, and why you feel you need to give it. Then ask for delivery advice.

> My partner yet again made us over an hour late to an important get-together at my workplace. She spends so much time getting ready and always starts at the last minute—it's very chaotic getting out the door. I hate being late, especially when it makes me look bad at work. When I've shared this with her in the past, she gets defensive. How can I deliver this feedback in a way that makes her listen and hopefully change these habits?

INTERPRET GENERATIONAL SLANG

New lingo seems to pop up every year, and sometimes it feels like learning a whole new language. When faced with a turn of phrase you don't understand, share with your AI tool the phrase, the age of the person who said it, and the context in which it was said. You can even create a "translation guide" to common lingo used by different generations.

> Create a robust guide to common words and phrases that have been adopted by Generation Z and Generation Alpha in the past few years. Detail the phrase, what it means, and how it might have originated. Then use it in a sentence or situation where the context is clear.

UNDERSTAND ETIQUETTE FOR DIFFERENT SITUATIONS

Understanding proper etiquette for unfamiliar situations ahead of time can help you know what to expect and avoid faux pas on the day of the event. Whether you are attending a cultural event that's new to you, a black-tie wedding, or just a very fancy dinner, ChatGPT can help you prepare and confidently participate.

> I've been invited to dinner at a very formal restaurant—one of those with elaborate place settings and multiple waiters per table. I really want to know what to expect, learn proper etiquette, and understand which utensil or glass to use and when! Please create a robust guide to address these questions and prepare me. Include any little-known tips as well as any actions to definitely avoid.

OVERCOME SOCIAL ANXIETY

If you struggle to engage at parties or in new groups of people, you can chat with ChatGPT about your anxieties and receive advice on how you might address them. You can also learn actionable tips for meeting new people at events and forming strong, fun, and memorable connections.

> I've just moved to a new city to start my graduate school program. I've been invited to a party for new master's students, and I feel anxious. I am very shy and hate small talk. I need you to (1) provide guidance for overcoming my

social anxiety, (2) suggest 5 interesting questions I can use when meeting new people that encourage deeper conversation, and (3) give me tips for gracefully exiting conversations that I am not enjoying.

INTERVIEW OLDER RELATIVES

Grandparents and parents hold a wealth of stories that their children and grandchildren have likely never heard. These stories can offer valuable and interesting insights into these loved ones while opening a door to new perspectives and gratitude for your current day-to-day life. ChatGPT can inspire unique questions for you to ask them over dinner or when visiting. If you want to take it even further, you can use ChatGPT's voice-to-text functionality to record their responses and ask the tool to transcribe their responses.

I am about to conduct an interview with my grandmother about her life. After this first message to you, I will send a transcription of each question from me and her recorded answers with each message. In response to each message, I would like you to transcribe my question and her answers word-for-word, tidying up with proper grammar and removing filler words like *ums* and *ahs*.

CHAPTER 9

Travel

Is it just me, or does travel (or at least the preparation for it) often feel like work? If you have a strong sense of wanderlust but have a hard time with the many logistics, considerations, and planning processes tied to vacationing, this chapter is for you. Like a great travel agent, ChatGPT can guide you through every stage of the travel planning process, from brainstorming and choosing your next destination to estimating costs and making recommendations for activities to do when you are there. It can save you a huge amount of time and mental burden so that you can focus on the *wander* and not the *I wonder*.

Even if you don't have much of a "travel bug," the prompts within this chapter will guide you in finding tactics and inspiration for exploring the world around you, even if it's close to home. From discovering exciting day trips for the family to uncovering little-known local gems, ChatGPT can provide recommendations near home and far away that provide relaxation, excitement, curiosity, and fun.

Forbes reported that the average American worker gets less than 12 days of paid vacation a year. And according to the US Travel Association, more than half of Americans don't even use all their paid time off. With ChatGPT, you'll feel more confident in your vacation choices, get a plan for every scenario, and have a lot of fun while there, all with a fraction of the effort you have previously spent planning vacations in the past. With all the mental energy you save, you may even be inspired to use all that PTO after all!

GET PERSONALIZED DESTINATION IDEAS

How AI Can Help You Pick Your Next Vacation

Most of us lead hectic lives with limited paid vacation days, but the cost and logistics of travel planning can feel overwhelming. Plus, our social feeds are filled with the excursions of friends (or influencers) traveling to destinations far and wide, so the pressure to do something amazing is high. With so many options to pick from (and so many ways to get there), choosing just one destination for your next vacation can feel like a drain, not a fun, exciting proposition.

With AI, perhaps the most difficult decision of your vacation planning—choosing a destination—can be made in a fraction of the time. All it takes is one very specific prompt. My favorite things about leveraging ChatGPT this early in the travel decision-making process are the personalized recommendations it provides and the freedom to ask for exactly what you want.

Set Up Your Initial Request

While your first prompt can be as simple as "Give me a recommendation for 5 romantic vacation destinations," you'll find the best results (and ones that get you the most excited for selecting your next trip!) are those with lots of details. On a strict budget? No shame in calling that out. Seeking a nontraditional excursion that ignores the things you "should" do in a given location? ChatGPT isn't going to judge. Provide details on your vacation likes and dislikes, the amount of time you plan to be there, and any considerations when it comes to lodging or budget.

Sample Starter Prompt

Playing the role of an expert travel agent, give me 10 recommendations for a honeymoon vacation. Your recommendations should span destinations across continents. We have approximately 10 days for this trip. Some additional context: We love trying new foods, adventurous activities that are not overly dangerous, exploring fascinating nature and history, and taking in romantic views. We're also interested in staying in a luxurious hotel without paying luxurious prices.

Additional Ways to Personalize

Dive Deeper Into Each Destination

Once you've got some initial inspiration, you can ask ChatGPT to provide even more specific details on a few destinations you're considering. In your prompt, list the features you would like more information on so you can envision what a vacation might look like at a particular place. I recommend asking the tool to respond with details for one destination at a time, as this will make its responses more thorough, instead of trying to fit all explanations into one response.

> For each destination on your list, please detail specifically why honeymooners like us might love this destination. Include (1) an overview of the destination's cuisine worth trying, (2) why it's a good place for romance, and (3) a list of 5 must-do activities that you think we will enjoy if we travel to this destination. Do these one at a time, starting with Santorini.

Recommend the Best Time of Year to Visit

If you are trying to determine both a destination *and* a time for your next vacation, ChatGPT can guide you in understanding the pros and cons of visiting any location as a tourist during different times of the year. With the following prompt, you'll understand in detail what certain months or seasons will look and feel like. You can also ask about very specific things you like or dislike when traveling, like if you want to avoid crowds or if certain weather ruins your vacation experience. ChatGPT will consider these in its response.

> For each destination, I want you to share the best months or seasons in the year to consider visiting. One destination at a time, please highlight 2–3 months for each destination (all from different seasons), and explain

why I might enjoy traveling to that destination during that month, and also why I might not. Keep in mind: (1) I want to avoid rain on my vacation, (2) I enjoy interesting cultural experiences that one can only experience as a tourist at certain times of the year, and (3) I enjoy cost savings on travel and lodging. We'll start with Kyoto now.

Get Ideas for Destinations Closer to Home

If you have a shorter time to enjoy on vacation or have other circumstances (like an expired passport!) keeping you within your home country, ChatGPT can suggest destinations or lesser-known cities to visit. By asking about these within the same chat, you don't even need to list all your previously mentioned travel preferences—ChatGPT will remember what is relevant to you.

We're also considering a mini-moon for a long weekend after our wedding. We live in Atlanta, Georgia, and want to keep our mini-moon closer to home. Please recommend 6 lesser-known cities in the United States that we might enjoy visiting for a shorter period based on what you already know about our preferences, and detail why you'd recommend them for our mini-moon.

CREATE AN ITINERARY

How AI Can Plan Your Time Away

Are you a fan of strict schedules? Or do you just want a little inspiration for a few things to do on an upcoming trip? Asking ChatGPT to create an itinerary for your upcoming trip will save you hours of brainstorming and planning. And the best part? The output will be perfectly customized to your needs. Even if you aren't a fan of a strict schedule, the process of making itineraries with AI can inspire further research on what to do while there, while also giving you a good understanding of what activities to group together.

Set Up Your Initial Request

When crafting your prompt, start with the basics: Where are you going, for how long, and what would you like to do while there? Add details about who you are traveling with (partner, kids, etc.). It's also helpful to include details on the time of year you are traveling and the types of activities you enjoy. If there are "must-do" activities you absolutely want included, list those as well. If you'd like a lot of details for your itinerary, like in-depth descriptions of recommended activities or places to eat, request the itinerary be generated one day at a time. Leave out that request for a less in-depth schedule.

Sample Starter Prompt

You're an expert travel agent. Please craft a 7-day, 6-night London itinerary for my family's August trip. I need you to write this out 1 day at a time, starting with day 1. Include suggested activities like things to do and see and places to eat. We are interested in history, the arts, and must-see landmarks and experiences. All activities should be appropriate for kids ages 10 and 14, while also enjoyable for adults. In your itinerary, please ensure minimal travel time, while favoring a relaxed pace, and highlight landmarks to see each day based on the location of recommended activities.

Additional Ways to Personalize

Get Details on Prices in Your Itinerary

After ChatGPT has made your itinerary, you may be wondering, "How much is this trip going to cost?" To get a rough estimate of the costs for all activities and dining options for each day in your itinerary, use this prompt. While costs may not be exact, they will be a good estimate of roughly what to expect if you book these activities.

For all of the activities you listed in my itinerary, could you provide an esti-mated cost per person to participate in each one, based on historical prices? Please format this with "Day #," then "<Activity Name> $X person."

Create a Road Trip Itinerary

If you like to pack your vacations with visits to multiple cities but hate the logistics of figuring out where to go, how long to stay, and what to do while you're there (or where to stop along the way), a simple AI prompt can save you a *lot* of mental energy. Even if the only things you can supply are your starting and ending destination and the maximum amount of time you want to spend in a car, ChatGPT can plan a stellar road trip.

I'm planning a 20-day road trip from Greenville, SC, to Los Angeles, CA. I need your help suggesting a route that ensures that I'm never driving more than 5 hours in a day, giving me enough time to experience a bit of each city or place as I go. I want to see diverse landscapes, natural parks, major cities, and scenic routes.

Get Recommendations for Stops Along Your Route

You can then leverage follow-up prompts to adjust your road trips' recom-mended route to your heart's content. Once you've landed on a path you like, you can get inspiration for things to do along the way.

Based on the route you provided, please suggest specific stops and attractions along the way. I'm interested in historical sites, natural parks, and unique local attractions.

Find Places to Stay Along the Way

Especially for longer road trips or ones where you may be hauling a moving truck or trailer with you, finding comfortable accommodations that fit your unique parking needs can be difficult. AI can help with this as well! If you want a couple of options per stop, it's helpful to ask for recommendations for just a few nights at a time. This will allow ChatGPT to go into a bit more detail for each suggestion.

> For each main stop on the road trip, please recommend 2–3 comfortable and affordable (less than $150/night) accommodations located near or between each stop on the route. We are driving a large U-Haul truck, so it's important that these locations allow for such vehicles and have good security. Recommend places for the first 3 stops first, and detail their star rating and a rough estimate of the price of the stay.

Plan a Round-Trip Road Trip

If you're flying into and out of the same airport (or starting and ending at your own home), but you want to drive through a number of different places once you've arrived, ChatGPT can recommend a route for these types of road trips. In your prompt, detail the goals of your trip, including any cities you are hoping to pass through, and ask ChatGPT to suggest an optimized route that has you hitting all your target stops while spending as little time in the car as possible.

> You're an expert travel agent specializing in road trips that are memorable and efficient, maximizing time spent exploring and minimizing time in the car. I would like you to help me plan a 10-day road trip through major cities in Spain and Portugal, starting and ending in Madrid, and passing through Lisbon.

DISCOVER ACTIVITIES AT YOUR DESTINATION

How AI Can Research Things to Do While There

Instead of spending hours combing through search engine results only to end up with a disorganized page of handwritten notes or a brain dump in a Word document, enlist AI to organize all of the things you can do into a tidy table format so you can easily compare and contrast options and pick what's best for you.

Set Up Your Initial Request

With ChatGPT, you can create a table of just about anything! In your prompt, all you'll need to include is the phrase "Make a table of <table category>" and specifics on what columns you would like in your table. The magic of the table prompt comes in when you detail what data (columns) you would like included for each item on your list. Examples of data include the name of the activity, a brief description of the activity, the cost per person, the category of activity (arts, history, culture, outdoor adventure, etc.), how far away it is from your hotel or a nearby landmark, and the estimated time it'll take to get there. For inspiration, I like to start broad in category, then narrow down for more specifics. When ChatGPT finishes your table, you can continue to build on it by simply saying: "Add more rows/columns."

Sample Starter Prompt

Make a table of activities and excursions for first-time tourists visiting Puerto Rico. We like accessible outdoor adventure activities that we can enjoy without needing to be super athletic, as well as nature, the arts, interesting culture and history, and good food and drinks. The columns in the table should be "Name of Activity," "Description of Activity," "Category of Activity" (outdoor adventure, arts, food, etc.), "Estimated Cost per Person," and approximate "Distance in Miles" from Río Grande, Puerto Rico.

Learn about Must-Do Tourist Activities

Every destination is known for something, but that something may not be the primary thing you are traveling for. Still, you don't want to miss a memorable opportunity just because you don't know about it! ChatGPT can be a great guide in pointing you toward those landmarks, activities, and foods that your destination is most known for. Try this prompt to make sure you are aware of any "must-do!" activities for your next vacation.

You are an expert travel guide who has recommended Washington, DC, as a fun, family-friendly destination to many clients whose kids are studying American history in school. Please create a guide to the top 10 "must-do" activities and landmarks or places that families traveling to DC should visit. We are first-time travelers to this city, so please detail why tourists love each recommendation in your response.

Learn about Must-Try Local Cuisines

ChatGPT is a great source of knowledge when it comes to what food a particular destination is known for, not only providing guidance on "must-try" dishes but also listing details on their ingredients and how they are typically prepared. It can also give you educational backstories on how the dish came to be and its history and evolution over time. While that information is not necessary to enjoy the food, it can make the experience of trying it for the first time all the more memorable.

I'm traveling to Lima, Peru, this May and want to sample multiple "must-try" cultural cuisines while there, both food and drink. But I really don't know much about what these are! Please create a guide outlining 10 dishes or drinks Lima, Peru, is known for, giving the name of each dish, a detailed description of the dish, and any fun facts about the dish and/or its history.

Discover Hidden Gems and Local Favorites

If you prefer avoiding places all the tourists flock to, or if you are visiting a favorite destination for a second or third time and just want to discover something new about it, ChatGPT can provide you with details on local favorites. From dining to activities, you'll quickly learn about off-the-beaten-path experiences so you can enjoy the area like the locals do.

> You are a local in Singapore who is knowledgeable about the cultural scene, including the best places to dine, exciting nightlife excursions, and unique places to experience the arts. You provide recommendations not typically highlighted in travel guides for tourists. In fact, you help people avoid tourist crowds! Please provide suggestions for my friend and me, 2 women in our 20s, for places to go and things to see to get a true taste of life lived in Singapore.

Plan for Seasonal Events and Experiences

Many destinations host unique experiences and activities tied specifically to certain times of the year, like the Christmas Markets of Berlin, Mardi Gras in New Orleans, or Gion Matsuri in Kyoto. If you have an upcoming vacation planned, you might be curious about whether there are any well-known cultural events or festivals happening while you're there. Get answers by providing ChatGPT with a simple prompt including details on your travel dates.

> I will be traveling through Spain for 2 weeks in March, and I am trying to figure out what cities I might visit. Are there any cool seasonal events or festivals happening around that time of year in Spain?

Discover Upcoming Events

By using an AI with access to web browsing, you can quickly summarize information on unique upcoming events at your chosen destination. For using AI to research unique limited-time events and activities for your chosen dates, I recommend waiting to use this prompt until a few weeks to a month before your travel dates to minimize AI hallucination.

Could you identify 10 upcoming events or performances in and around Phila-
delphia's music, arts, or nightlife scenes in May 2025? Make note of the date
they are happening and provide a brief description of the event.

Find Free or Low-Cost Activities

Whether you are on a tight budget or just love a good deal, ChatGPT and
AI tools can be excellent guides in pointing out all the varied free and low-cost
activities you can enjoy near your home or at your travel destination. In your
prompt, simply specify your budget and ask the AI tool to give you an estimate
of the total cost based on historical prices.

You are an expert in low-cost, budget-friendly travel. Please make a table
of free activities or activities at a cost of less than around $15 per person
(based on historical prices) in Edinburgh, Scotland. All activities should
be suitable for a family with a 12-year-old. In the table, make the columns
"Activity," "Price per Person," "Description of Activity," and "Why Tourists
Love the Activity."

GET "KNOW-BEFORE-YOU-GO" DETAILS

**How AI Can Help You Learn Key Facts
about Your Destination**

Being informed of local customs, transportation options and rules, safety tips,
cultural etiquette, and emergency procedures can enhance your travel experience by putting your mind at ease, knowing you are prepared for anything,
however unlikely it may be. ChatGPT can give you that information in a fraction of the time it would take to collect it on your own, ensuring you will spend
as little time as possible thinking about the less fun part of travel preparation.

Set Up Your Initial Request

While you *can* ask for everything at once in your first prompt, doing so will result in the "CliffsNotes" version for everything. I've found it's better to dedicate a single prompt to each know-before-you-go category after starting more simply with a basic guide. In your prompt, explain where you are headed, what time of year you are traveling, and some details on the area where you are staying. By starting with a simpler guide, you'll capture the *most* important "must-knows" so you don't find yourself thinking, "I should have known that!"

Sample Starter Prompt

> Make a "know-before-you-go" guide for my upcoming trip, tackling the most pertinent information first-time tourists regret not knowing in retrospect. I am visiting São Paulo, Brazil, in late April and staying in the Jardins area.

Additional Ways to Personalize

Research Transportation Options

Planning transportation at your destination can be particularly tedious. Understanding your options for getting around (and their relative costs) ahead of time can make everything go more smoothly. With ChatGPT's help, you can also take into account the context of where you plan to go once you're there. You may even learn about options you didn't know existed! In your prompt, detail where you are headed and what you plan to do while there to get advice on different modes of travel.

> I'm planning a trip to Paris, France, and staying near the Eiffel Tower. My travel bucket list includes day trips to visit Aix-en-Provence and Versailles, as well as exploring various destinations around Paris like the Louvre, the Arc de Triomphe, and Notre-Dame. Given this plan, I need your help to figure out the best transportation options while there, including suggestions for the most cost-effective ways to travel for my day trips. Is renting a car worth it?

What other transportation options can be used by tourists? I'm interested in efficient, straightforward, and low-cost options.

Create a Guide for Safe Travel

Ensuring a truly stress-free vacation involves an extra step of planning many of us don't like thinking about: what safety precautions you may need to take as a tourist in an unfamiliar place. Instead of reading horror stories online or throwing caution to the wind entirely, let AI provide you with an overview of the most important safety tips to know while traveling somewhere new.

My family will be visiting Marrakesh, Morocco, as part of our summer vacation. I want to ensure a safe and enjoyable experience. To help me prepare, could you provide a detailed guide on general safety tips for American travelers in Marrakesh?

Be Prepared for an Emergency Abroad

While it's not fun to think about, the possibility of facing an emergency situation when away from home is not unheard of—especially when you are traveling to an unfamiliar country where you may not know the language. Understanding ahead of time what to do or where to go in the event of a medical emergency or any other kind of crisis is valuable knowledge to have. AI can save you time on research by providing you with a quick overview of what you need to know.

I'll be traveling solo to Buenos Aires, Argentina, soon. I want to know exactly where to go, how to get help, and what number to call in the event of a medical emergency or any other kind of crisis. Please create a guide detailing what to do in the event of a medical emergency or any kind of crisis that could impact tourists abroad, including contact info for such emergencies and tips for these situations. Also detail what I should know about hospitals, pharmacies, or medical consultations in the event I get sick or need help.

Understand Cultural Sensitivities

When you are traveling to an unfamiliar country where the cultural norms and behaviors are very different from what you are used to, it can be helpful to understand these norms to avoid both potential embarrassment and disrespecting others. With ChatGPT, you can craft a guide to cultural norms and expectations to allow you to blend more naturally into your new surroundings and not stand out so prominently as a tourist.

My wife and I will be traveling to Cairo, Egypt, for an upcoming vacation. Please create a thorough guide to key social norms and cultural sensitivities that we may not be aware of as American citizens so that we can engage respectfully with locals and avoid embarrassment or standing out too obviously as tourists. In particular, detail if there are any hand gestures, expressions, or tendencies that mean something very different in Egypt than in America.

Understand Essential Etiquette in Foreign Countries

Etiquette can overlap with cultural sensitivities, but not always. Whether you want to understand how dining or tipping etiquette may be different from your home country or what kind of greeting is expected when meeting a local, ChatGPT can create an enlightening, educational, and helpful guide. In your prompt, detail where you are going, what culture or country you are coming from, and for what situations you need advice.

I'm visiting Tokyo, Japan, from the US and want to embrace local customs respectfully. Could you brief me on essential etiquette, from greeting and tipping norms to dining manners and restaurant behaviors? Include public behavior tips, like while using transit, and anything else I should be aware of. Aim for guidance that helps me blend in and respect traditions, ensuring a positive experience.

MAKE A RECOMMENDED PACKING LIST

How AI Can Help You Pack for Your Trip

Packing for your trip can present different challenges for different people, whether it's overpacking, under packing, or just forgetting critical items that you only notice are missing once you arrive. ChatGPT can help you determine the types and quantities of clothing to pack for your upcoming trip and can also provide recommendations for things you might otherwise overlook.

Set Up Your Initial Request

Start by providing ChatGPT with your length of stay, chosen destination, activities you'll be participating in, and time of year you'll be traveling, and request that it list the clothing items you should consider packing. Once you've got a thorough list of apparel, you can move on to other pertinent items to pack.

Sample Starter Prompt

I am a woman traveling to Puerto Rico for a 7-day, 6-night trip this April, and I need your help making a packing list for my trip. To start, just focus on all of the specific clothing items I'll need (and the quantity of each thing I should bring). Ensure all are suitable for the weather that time of year and the activities in which I'll be participating. These activities include a horseback ride, a hike through the rainforest, swimming, kayaking, nice dinners out, and general time spent at the resort.

Additional Ways to Personalize

Get a List of Non-Clothing Items

Next, ask ChatGPT to make a thorough list of all non-clothing items you will likely need to pack for your trip. In your prompt, emphasize the importance of being thorough and avoiding the risk of forgetting a critical item and having to disrupt your vacation to find it.

> Now continue my packing list for the trip, detailing all non-apparel items I could possibly need for my trip, including must-haves and what some might consider nonessential (but many find very valuable) considering the time of year, destination, and activities planned for the trip. I do not want to find myself in a situation where I need to purchase something I've forgotten, so please be thorough.

Verify Anything That May Be Missing

If you want to veer on the side of caution and make sure your packing list truly accounts for everything you might possibly need while away, send this simple prompt to ChatGPT. It may repeat some of what was already on your first packing list, but it will also come up with a few new, more niche items that you might actually find incredibly useful on your trip.

> Is there anything else I might be missing from the lists above that I should consider bringing?

Transcribe and Organize Your Dictated Packing List

Alternatively, if you know exactly what you need to pack for your trip but it all lives inside your head, ChatGPT can help you quickly jot down, sort, and nicely organize your list of items you are considering bringing. Just tap the little "microphone" icon in your app and dictate this prompt followed by a brain dump of all of the things you need to pack. This can be particularly helpful if you find yourself responsible for helping others in your family pack. By giving them a checklist to work off of, you can outsource at least some of that physical work by dictating the strategy, and save time writing everything down.

> My family is preparing for a week-long skiing trip in Denver, Colorado, this February. I need your help organizing a list of things my teenage son needs to remember to pack so that I can give him a clear list to work off

of. I'm going to ramble off the top of my head all of the things he should pack. Once I've finished, first make a categorically organized packing list from what I've told you, then suggest any items I may be forgetting. Here's what he needs to pack: <Ramble off everything on your mind.>

GET TRANSLATION ASSISTANCE ABROAD

How AI Can Act As Your Translator

Going somewhere where the primary language is not one you speak? Good news: With your ChatGPT app, you've got an always-on pocket translator. ChatGPT and other AI tools can understand, translate, and write in countless languages, including Spanish, French, Italian, German, Dutch, Chinese, Japanese, Korean, and Arabic. The more popular the language, the more likely that AI will be fluent in it (fluency depends on how much text in that language is in its training data). Even for world languages that it has less robust training data on, ChatGPT can still create reliable basic translation guides for English-speaking tourists visiting those countries.

Set Up Your Initial Request

Knowing how to say just 10–15 key phrases can be immensely helpful while traveling in a country where you don't speak the local language. Such phrases can enable you to respectfully greet locals, ask them for help when necessary, and more easily navigate your surroundings. I like the table format best for this response, as it can give you a clear side-by-side breakdown of the phrase, its translation, and its phonetic pronunciation.

I am traveling to the Czech Republic as a tourist who only speaks English. Please provide me with a translation guide to common phrases that will be helpful for me to know while there, ranging from greetings to emergency phrases, words of thanks, asking for help, ordering food, and seeking directions. Please format this guide as a table, where the columns are "English Phrase," "Translation," and "Phonetic Pronunciation."

Additional Ways to Personalize

Make Translation Guides for Specific Scenarios

Now that you've got some basic phrases that cover a wide variety of scenarios, in the prompts that follow, you can dig even deeper. You might request short translation guides catered to specific scenarios, like dining out, asking for directions, or emergency situations.

Now create a more specific guide for phrases that could help me in a situation where I am dining out at a restaurant.

Translate Language from a Photo

Now that you know AI can be a great translator, you may be thinking, "Oh! So, if I see something in another language, I could just type it into ChatGPT and have it translated for me!" You are correct. However, it gets better than that! Generative AI tools with vision capabilities (where you can upload an image) can also "see" text in an uploaded photo and translate it from there. So if you see a sign you can't understand or need some help translating a menu, just snap a photo on your phone and upload it into your AI chat with the following prompt.

Attached is a picture of a menu at a restaurant I am eating at. Please translate the menu into English.

Get a Live Translation

Believe it or not, you can use ChatGPT's free app to serve in a pinch as a live audio translator if you are engaging with someone who speaks a language other than your own. To start with your translation, just give ChatGPT the following prompt. After that, whenever you or the other person needs to say something, tap the "microphone" icon in your ChatGPT app to record their words, send it to your new "translator," and watch as it translates their phrases into English and vice versa. Finally, once you've got your translation in the app, instead of making the other person read your translated text, you can press your finger on the translation (with a long hold), then select "Read aloud" for ChatGPT to read the translation aloud to them!

I need you to act as a translator between myself (speaking English) and another person (who speaks Spanish). From here on out, when you hear a phrase in English, I need you to translate the exact words directly into Spanish. When you hear a phrase in Spanish, I need you to translate the exact words back into English. Got it? We'll begin with my next prompt.

LEARN MONEY-SAVING TIPS FOR TOURISTS

Tourists often spend more money than they need to on activities, food, and transportation. If only you knew what the locals knew about safe and inexpensive travel options, delicious affordable restaurants, or fun and free events and excursion! With AI, you can learn all this in a matter of seconds. It can even give you details about special discounts you may qualify for, like student or teacher prices.

> My friend and I are visiting New York City as tourists for the first time! We are students hoping to find ways to enjoy all the city has to offer while not overspending. Please create a thorough guide to the best tips and tricks for saving money as tourists in New York that only the locals know. Include a list of any attractions offering student discounts.

GET TIPS FOR OVERCOMING JET LAG

Red-eye flights are often one of the most economical choices when traveling to a country far away. If you can manage to fight through the fatigue after you arrive, this can also be a way to rapidly adjust to the new time zone. To avoid the magnetic pull of your hotel bed, use ChatGPT to help make a plan of action in advance to sleep better on the plane, fight through jet lag, and adjust to your new time zone.

> This July, my family is traveling from Dallas, Texas, to Vienna, Austria, on a red-eye flight arriving at around 11:30 a.m., Austria time. We are staying at a hotel in the Inner City, where our check-in time is 3:00 p.m. I need you to create a guide on (1) what to do near our hotel to keep us awake and active until at least 10:00 p.m. and (2) how to combat jet lag generally and adjust to a new time zone. Give me specific proven advice as well as little-known tips.

LEARN TO RECOGNIZE SIGNS AND TRAFFIC RULES ABROAD

Understanding street signs and traffic symbols isn't a typical part of the travel planning process, but once you arrive in a new country where the symbols are unfamiliar or the streets are difficult to navigate, you may wish it had been!

ChatGPT can help you understand key signage that helps you navigate better, stay safe, and find your way. If you are renting a car, it will also be very helpful to understand traffic patterns and what to expect as a driver in a new city.

> I am an American visiting Madrid, Spain, and I want to be able to understand how to navigate the city while there as both a pedestrian and driver. I need you to create a guide to local street and traffic signs, pedestrian signals, and common signs for things like pharmacies, water fountains, and public transit. Please describe what the signs look like and what they mean, and provide any additional tips you have for efficiently navigating the city on foot and by car.

TAKE A SELF-GUIDED TOUR

Did you know AI can function as an always-on tour guide? When on vacation, whenever a statue, building, or anything else catches your interest, snap a clear photo with your phone and upload it into your AI tool with vision capabilities to give you information about it. When you upload your photo, add extra context on your location to help the vision feature identify the object of interest, then do a quick search of the identified object to see if it's right! From there, ask any follow-up questions you have.

> Please help me identify the brick building in the attached image. This building was taken in the downtown Boston area. My picture doesn't clearly show it, but there is a statue of a golden lion on the top left of the building and a golden unicorn on the top right. What could I be looking at and what can you tell me about it?

ESTIMATE TIME TO SPEND ON ACTIVITIES

When planning your trip or weekend, it can be very useful to understand how much time you should dedicate to your activity of choice. ChatGPT can help you understand what to expect and provide guidance on what to prioritize if you find yourself with limited time. If the activity is farther away, ChatGPT can share how you might get to your destination and the estimated time and cost to get there depending on your method of travel.

> My family and I want to visit Windsor Castle during our upcoming trip to London. We are staying near the Tower Bridge. I need your help with a handful of things: (1) detail the different ways we should consider getting to the castle, with estimated costs, time spent traveling, and pros and cons for each, and (2) recommend how much time we should spend in Windsor and justify your recommendation.

GET INSIDER TIPS FOR THEME PARK VISITS

Is your family planning a trip to a major theme park destination soon? You'll likely find that the ins and outs of a successful and stress-free trip at major theme parks may not be as straightforward as it once was, with heavy crowds, special digital apps and ride queuing considerations, "fast passes," and other details. There's delicious food to eat, rides to line up for, shows to see, and so much more! If you are not a regular visitor, it can all feel overwhelming. AI tools, especially those with web-browsing functionality, can help by summarizing some must-knows into a guide and answering any follow-up questions.

> My family is taking a 5-day trip to Disney World, and we are trying to determine how best to optimize our time across the four parks as well as finding tips for avoiding crowds and seeing the main attractions while minimizing time waiting in lines. We're also hoping to enjoy some of the best Disney treats while there. Please create a guide of considerations and insider tips to getting the most out of our time at the parks. We have never been before as a family and do not know how passes, tickets, and ride queuing work, so please be as detailed as possible.

PLAN ACTIVITIES FOR RAINY DAYS

Don't let your vacation get spoiled by a rainy day! Whether you like to plan for bad weather in advance or deal with it as it happens, ChatGPT can help you come up with an alternative fun plan, fast.

> Help! I just learned my family's vacation in Miami, Florida, will be disrupted by heavy rainfall for 3 of our 5 days there. Please help me come up with a robust list of family-friendly things to do in and around the

Miami area that can be enjoyed, rain or shine. We have a car and are willing to drive an hour out of the city.

GET SUGGESTIONS FOR OUTDOOR EXPLORATION

While you may have chosen your destination for reasons outside of exploring nature, many vacations can be enhanced by spending an afternoon taking in the natural wonders of a location. Not only are these types of excursions typically free; you can also discover incredible views while marveling at interesting flora and fauna when you venture out to explore outside of the typical tourist spots. And of course, these types of prompts can be used while traveling and in your hometown alike!

> Please suggest 10 excursions in nature that I could try within 45 minutes of Edinburgh that I could reach by walking and public transit and perhaps a short rideshare. List what makes the adventure special, if anything, as well as details on how to get to each place.

GET INSPIRATION FOR AND PLAN A DAY TRIP FROM HOME

Whether you're looking to just get away from home for a quick Saturday excursion or you're hoping to explore hidden gems during your vacation, ChatGPT can be a great partner in learning about fun day excursions. For this prompt, you'll want to specify how far you are willing to travel (and by what means of transport), the approximate time you'd like to depart, and when you'd like to return. You may also detail whether you are hoping to experience one lengthier activity on your day trip or a series of smaller explorations.

> Help me come up with and plan a memorable Saturday day trip for my 12-year-old daughter and me, her father. We are in Charlotte, North Carolina, and I would like to drive no more than 3 hours one way and return home by nightfall. She enjoys arts and crafts, animals, and nature. Give me 5 ideas, detailing the length of the drive, things to do once there, and any tips on stops along the route to break the trip up and create more memories.

CHAPTER 10

Fun and Entertainment

Since OpenAI's launch, "fun" hasn't been the main topic the media has covered—but it's a great reason to use the tool! There is something so imaginative and miraculous about working with a tool that can understand, interact, and engage with you in a creative way. From playing word games, to crafting interactive stories, to creating and inspiring works of art, AI tools have the power to bring more fun and joy to your life.

In this chapter, we'll cover dozens of ways to entertain yourself and others with AI, at work, at home, with friends, or when alone. Prompts in this chapter give you an optimal opportunity to employ the "temperature" tip mentioned in Part 1 of this book. To generate even more inventive explorations from your chats when using ChatGPT or Copilot, include higher temperatures at the end of your prompt (like 0.9 and 1.0).

ENTERTAIN CHILDREN

How AI Can Help You Entertain Children

The dreaded "I'm bored" or "But I'm not tired!" announcements from kids are a struggle for parents everywhere. Let AI help you think of fun ideas for delightful storytelling, screen-free entertainment, family dinner topics, and more when you're too busy or exhausted yourself.

Set Up Your Initial Request

The next time your child is pining for a story, leverage AI to instantly create something custom, incorporating unique characters your kids will love and even adding a little something for yourself—a special "moral of the story" that may drive home a lesson you'd like your kids to learn. Include your child's age and any details on the types of characters or the setting you'd like. You can even let your child guide some inputs to make this practice more interactive! You can personalize even more requests for different writing styles (like "rhyming") or certain plot points.

Sample Starter Prompt

I need your help crafting a memorable bedtime story for my 5-year-old son. The main character in the story should learn a valuable lesson by the end. My son is very into bugs at the moment.

Additional Ways to Personalize

Create Illustrations for Your Story

Want to take the fun of your story even further? By using an AI with image-generation capabilities, you can create a fun series of images to accompany your story. Start your prompt with the command to "Make an image" and then request the ultimate style for the image that your child would like.

Watercolor? Comic book? Disney 2-D animation? Finally, detail what should be in the image. You can also just give your tool a scene from the story and ask it to illustrate that!

> Please make an image that illustrates this scene from the story: <Scene.>
> The style should be a whimsical and colorful illustration style with a variety of textures and sketch lines.

Evolve Your Image and Scene

When AI image-generation features are incorporated into AI tools with natural language processing, you can actually continue to speak conversationally to your tool about how it should adjust or evolve your image. For example, if the main character from your story was featured in the first image you created, you can request your next image to include the same character but in a different setting or doing a different thing.

> Now make an image showing the same character (the little boy in the previous picture), but now the boy is running up a hill at night, with a crescent moon shining in the background. He carries a backpack. Maintain the same Pixar style.

Create a Coloring Page

Your child can continue to engage with their custom bedtime story beyond bedtime when you transform a scene from the story into a coloring book page! You can also request a custom coloring book page yourself for any scene. Just detail the specifics of the subject of the image, emphasize a white background and bold black lines with a lot of negative space.

> Now take this image and turn it into a simple coloring book page consisting of bold black lines outlining the scene over a white background. The lines should outline the character and scene and occasionally add texture, but the majority of the page should be white so that it can be colored in.

Get Seasonal Craft Ideas

If your kids are bored during the day, what about finding a fun craft to do with them? ChatGPT can instantly generate great ideas for age-appropriate crafts no matter the season or occasion. Detail the ages of your children, the season or holiday you'd like to consider for your craft, and perhaps how involved you'd like it to be. Will the craft take 10 minutes or an hour? What is the maximum number of materials you'd like it to require? Once you've got your ideas, just follow up with step-by-step instructions and a materials list.

> Generate 10 fun and easy craft ideas inspired by the fall season that are appropriate for a 6-year-old child. The crafts should take no more than 45 minutes for a 6-year-old to complete. They should require minimal adult supervision and be relatively mess-free.

Ideas for Age-Appropriate Entertainment Around the House

If you are tired of seeing your kids in front of tablets, TVs, or video games, turn to ChatGPT for ideas on screen-free DIY science experiments, outdoor adventures, simple DIY games, and other memorable activities. Detail the level of parental involvement, the time you'd like the activity to take up, and whether you have certain materials on hand you'd like to use (like old streamers, party balloons, etc.).

> Help me generate 10 ideas to entertain my 3-year-old at home this afternoon using materials likely already found in my home. These ideas should be unique, specific, engaging, and at least somewhat active despite having to be inside, as it is raining today.

Create a Mad Libs Template

Mad Libs, the silly and fun fill-in-the-blanks game, has been entertaining kids since the series was first published many decades ago. In addition to being fun, these fill-in-the-blanks–style stories can be valuable in teaching your kids the different parts of speech (noun, verb, etc.). With ChatGPT, you can easily create your own custom Mad Libs game, themed to whatever subject your kids find compelling. Create your game, get a pencil and paper to write down their responses, then have a blast reading the final result aloud together!

> Make a silly Mad Lib–style template that a 10-year-old would enjoy. It should include plenty of fill-in-the-blanks to customize the story (multiple per sentence). Fill-in-the-blanks words should be adjectives, nouns, actions, adverbs, and so on. The whole Mad Lib should be approximately 300 words.

Generate Family-Focused "Would You Rather?" Questions

A fun way to ignite lively discussion is a classic game of "Would You Rather?" In this game, the group is presented with two distinct but balanced scenarios, asked to pick one, and defend their answer. ChatGPT can generate an endless list of scenarios to consider for your game, tailored to the age levels you are playing with, or to particular themes or topics your kids interesting. By adding a higher "temperature" (1.0 being the highest) to the end of your prompt, the variety and randomness of questions generated will increase!

> Generate 20 questions for a game of "Would You Rather?" that are appropriate for families to play with an 8-year-old and 12-year-old. The scenarios presented should be specific and interesting. Some should be funny, some gross, some serious, and some thought-provoking. Temperature 1.0.

Inspire Fun Dinner Table Conversations

We all lead such busy lives that family dinnertime may seem fleeting. And with all the distractions available, when you do spend time sitting around the table with your family, sometimes you might just sit in silence while you eat or only ask the boring "How was your day?" and get back equally simple answers. ChatGPT can enliven your time together with interesting questions demanding more than simple one-word questions.

I want to maximize time around the dinner table with my wife and teenagers by asking more interesting questions and getting everyone engaged in conversation. Can you suggest 20 varied, unique, thought-provoking questions that might actually be interesting enough for a teenager to want to answer and discuss?

MAKE WORK MORE FUN

How AI Can Help Introduce Fun to the Workplace

To quote Mary Poppins, "In every job that must be done, there is an element of fun. You find the fun, and—SNAP—the job's a game!" While I can't guarantee ChatGPT can turn *every* workday into one filled with laughter and fun, it can certainly get you partially there, providing you with new opportunities to spark joy, enjoy a chuckle, and foster stronger relationships with your coworkers.

Whether you are joining a new team or hoping to reinvigorate an existing one, team-building activities, however small or simple, can help form stronger team bonds and even inspire more creativity in group problem-solving. With ChatGPT's help, you can generate ideas for engaging team activities suitable for both in-person and virtual environments.

Set Up Your Initial Request

Start by sharing with ChatGPT a little about the rough makeup of your team, what challenges you might be facing that you're hoping this exercise may help you overcome, and how much time you have to dedicate to the activity. Also detail the required setting—does it need to be conducive to a virtual environment? Or are you located in an office or even enjoying being off-site at a certain location? Additional helpful context could also be your team's function in the company.

I am on a fully remote team of 7 people. I can tell everyone has been feeling the burden of an ultraheavy workload lately. Our weekly meetings start off in silence, and we all seem even more drained by the end. In our next meeting, I want to bring back our groove with a fun team-building activity or game that can be done easily in this virtual space. Give me 10 unique suggestions for such an activity suited for my team. Temperature 1.0.

Additional Ways to Personalize ○

Come Up with Icebreaker Questions

Short on time for an activity but still want to spend some time each week on team bonding? ChatGPT can help you come up with work-appropriate questions to better get to know your coworkers and add a little fun to work.

Give me 10 fun and original questions that could be posted to my teammates at work to answer. The goal is to enhance team bonding (without getting unnecessarily deep or too personal).

Spark Silly Debates

Giving your teammates a silly topic to debate can be a fun diversion during the workday while also introducing valuable practice in healthy debate and discussion. By giving ChatGPT examples of the kinds of questions you might be looking for in its output, you can empower it to be even more precise with its suggestions.

Give me 20 fun and original questions that could spark fun and high-spirited debates among my coworkers. These debates should not be on serious topics but rather silly topics that one could still debate with logic and reason. Some examples of what I'm looking for include: "Is a hotdog a sandwich?" "Is water wet?" "Are clowns funny or scary?"

Make Entertaining Meeting Recaps

A sneaky but silly way to encourage people to read the meeting notes? Get inventive with their structure or tone. Paste your recap into ChatGPT after a prompt telling it in what fun way you'd like the recap summarized. Should the key takeaways be written in the form of a movie script? Or maybe a country song? Or maybe Kermit the Frog should provide the recap? Keep them reading with a fun new scenario each time (and, for added clarity, do include your *actual* notes).

> Below in quotation marks are the key next steps and takeaways from a recent work meeting. Please rewrite all these key next steps and takeaways as a movie script featuring the Muppets. Here are the notes <paste your notes here>.

Add Fun Imagery to Presentations

Need a quick way to make internal presentations more compelling? Adding in a fun and quirky image can not only add life to a boring but necessary topic; it can also help you more easily illustrate a point in a meaningful way. Whereas in the past you might have spent a bit too much time finding the perfect image for your presentation, with AI, you can generate that image in less than a minute of your time!

> Make a funny image for a PowerPoint slide that illustrates the perils of not getting communications approved by the compliance department. The resulting image should depict a businessperson in a funny but extreme scenario.

Create Silly Zoom Backgrounds

Add a little more fun and personality to your meetings by making your own AI-generated Zoom backgrounds. There are a couple of approaches you can take here—with ChatGPT Plus, you can create horizontal images in a 16:9 aspect ratio directly. The free image-generation tools in Gemini and Copilot may limit you to square images that you could later crop. Another free image-generation tool is Ideogram, which will allow you to make your image in the 16:9 style. Want a funny sign in your Zoom background? Ideogram also specializes in adding readable text to images!

> Make an image in 16:9 dimensions suitable for a Zoom background. The image should be of a sci-fi/futuristic office setting, in a top-floor building overlooking a beautiful space city–inspired background.

LEARN ABOUT THE WORLD AROUND YOU

How AI Can Help Satisfy Your Curiosity

While on a nature walk, have you ever seen something you've never seen before, like a beautiful flower or unique bird? Or perhaps you learned in passing about a new concept, theory, or moment from history and want to learn more? Because of AI's incredible summarization ability, you can ask it very detailed questions to dive further into your topic of choice and receive concise and informative responses within seconds.

Set Up Your Initial Request

The next time you are on a stroll and see something you don't quite recognize, you can turn to your AI tool to identify it and unlock new knowledge. With a combination of an uploaded photograph of the object and a description of the context surrounding it (i.e., where you are located, perhaps what time of year it is, etc.), you'll soon learn what it might be.

Sample Starter Prompt

> Attached is a photo of a duck I just saw. I'm at a lake in North Carolina, and it's currently early April. I don't think these ducks are normally here throughout the year, so they must be migratory. Do you have any guesses of what they could be?

Troubleshoot with Further Detail

Once you've got your first answer, cross-reference the suggestion with a quick search in your favorite web browser. Did AI not get it quite right? Just like you would with a person, explain what it got right and where it went wrong. This back-and-forth is especially useful if you can't get a good photo. It's very possible to get to the right answer with a combination of context and correction alone!

> The duck you suggested has a browner head than the one I am observing. This duck has a dark blue or purple head, black tail feathers, and a brown body with really dark speckles all over it. Its head is interesting—on either side, there is a kind of a white crescent that goes in front of its eyes and along the line of its beak.

Understand Animal Behavior

Whether you spot something you've never seen before in nature or you just want to better understand your pet, AI can help you quickly answer any random questions you may have about animal behavior. Just detail what you've observed to ChatGPT and ask for further explanation.

> I just saw something I've never seen before on a hike! Two whitetail deer in a shallow creek, seemingly intentionally splashing in the water (pawing at the soft ground beneath), then circling each other while jumping back and forth and wagging their tails. They almost looked like dogs playing. Is this normal behavior? Do deer play? Or is this something else?

Explore Scientific Theories and Thought Experiments

Ever come across an interesting scientific theory or event that you wanted to learn more about? From quantum entanglement to the Fermi paradox, ChatGPT can help you break down complex theories, ideas, or explanations in ways that help you better understand the subject or topic, its merits, and perhaps even its criticisms.

I want to learn about quantum entanglement: What is it? What's its history in the scientific community? What are the basics I need to know? How is it thought of, both positively and negatively, by those who discuss it? Please explain in plain terms so that someone like me with little understanding of the subject can learn.

Answer Random Questions about History

Have you ever been watching a movie set in a historical period and wondered about a passing detail or referenced event? Understanding the nuances of the time and setting of a film can help you better appreciate and understand the story, and also understand where the artists behind it may have taken some liberties! With the help of AI, you can answer those random questions faster.

In the movie *Braveheart*, everyone's faces are painted blue for battle. How historically accurate is that?

Create New Visual Concepts and Ideas

You can also turn curiosity on its head and come up with your own unique objects, scenes, and worlds. If you enjoy exploring new ideas or visual concepts but aren't particularly artistically skilled, AI tools with image generation can unlock new possibilities for artistic creation. With AI image generation, just about anything can be visualized, all through the power of the words in your prompts!

Make an image of a steampunk jungle, where almost all the flora and fauna are mechanical. The animals commonly found in the jungle look like sleek robotic and mechanical versions of familiar rainforest animals.

HELP WITH GAME NIGHT

How AI Can Help with Game Night

If you are a fan of hosting friends for a classic game night, AI can be leveraged in a variety of ways to make both preparation and gameplay itself more efficient and fun. With AI, you can create more inventive prompts for games, craft new games to play, and avoid obstacles like missing instructions or game materials.

Set Up Your Initial Request

You have a lot of flexibility when crafting your prompts for games. Share with ChatGPT any and all details to get the necessary aid from it, like the type of game you want to play, the game materials you'd like it to provide, how many players there are, and so on. There is no sample starter prompt for this section because in most scenarios, a single initial prompt can result in quick success, and each prompt will vary based on your needs.

Additional Ways to Personalize

Generate Prompts for Charades or Pictionary

If you are a fan of classic games like Charades, Pictionary, or any games that ultimately require text prompts for players to use in play, ChatGPT can serve as a substitute for any formal game materials. It can even create prompts within a themed category if you request it in your prompt! Simply ask it to generate one phrase or word at a time so that when it's the next player's turn, they need only say "Go!" for their next secret word if they are at a loss as to what phrase to act out.

I need you to become a random prompt generator for a game of Charades. Whenever I say "Go!," you will generate a book, film, or song title for someone to use as their subject to act out in Charades. Only use real titles. Always indicate if it is a book, film, or song. Choose subjects that are generally well known.

Act As a Substitute for Missing Dice

Similarly, if you are pulling out a classic board game that requires dice or any random drawing of chance, but you notice a key piece—like the die—is missing, ChatGPT can serve as your number or letter randomizer in a pinch. Give it instructions like the following one in your prompt, while specifying what exactly it is replacing, like how many dice or what range of numbers or letters appear on your die. Then enjoy your game!

> I need you to randomly generate numbers 1 through 6 for 2 fake "dice" to help me replace the real dice I have lost. When I say "Go!," you will "roll the dice" and respond with a format of "Die One: [Number], Die Two: [Number]." The [Number] must be between 1 and 6 for each die.

Learn to Play a Complicated Card or Tile Game

Have you ever played a complicated card game taught to you by a friend and wanted to teach it to others, but you just can't quite remember all the rules? Or maybe there's a new complex game you are hoping to learn, but all the lengthy instructions and how-to videos just feel overwhelming. You just want to talk to a person and have them explain it! AI can help. Begin by asking it for an overview of gameplay, then ask it for further details if needed on the different parts of gameplay. Feeling stuck? Ask for further explanation, just like you would a friend who is explaining the rules of the game as you play.

> I recently purchased a mah-jongg set, but I am having trouble understanding how to play. Please explain gameplay to me thoroughly, from the different types of tiles and game structure, to how to deal and start the game, to how to play the game.

Create a Themed Trivia Game

A game of themed trivia can be a lot of fun for larger group gatherings, where your group can be split into smaller teams to compete against each other. But crafting a well-structured trivia game, with varying levels of difficulty and a bunch of strong questions, can be time-consuming. With the help of AI, you can rapidly generate ideas for questions, and their subsequent answers, for your game. Use AI's suggestions as a starting point, then be sure to check the phrasing of the questions and their associated questions for accuracy to avoid debate in the event of AI hallucinations, especially for more niche topics.

> I need your help creating a *Friends*-themed trivia game for my friends. There should be 4 rounds of 5 questions each, and each round should introduce progressively more tough questions. No questions should be "easy," though—all questions should be challenging for major fans of the series. Please provide all questions and their answers.

Make a Game of *Jeopardy!* for Guests to Play

If you and your friends are fans of *Jeopardy!*, AI can help you structure a complete *Jeopardy!* game, with categories, levels with "dollar" values, questions, answers, and multiple rounds in under a minute! You can even refine your prompt to suggest a more specific category for your whole game like "musical theater," "Marvel," or "American history." Or, after a game has been created, ask the tool to increase or decrease the difficulty level. More advanced AI models (like Claude 3.5 and GPT-4o) will perform these tasks better than their earlier models. As always, do a quick fact-check for all generated questions before starting your game.

> Please create a *Jeopardy!* game with 2 rounds (Jeopardy and Double Jeopardy) and a Final Jeopardy round. In your game, map out the categories, clues (like "The largest planet in our solar system"), and answers (in the form of questions, like "What is Jupiter?"), for each round. The game board should have the categories across the top row and the increasing dollar values as the rows. Every cell in the game board should contain both a clue and the answer to the clue formatted as follows: "Clue: <Clue>. Answer: <Answer>."

PLAY 1:1 GAMES WITH AI!

How AI Can Tackle Boredom with Gameplay

Stuck in line? Trouble falling asleep? Just looking for a little mind stimulation as you sip your morning coffee? Prompt AI to play a classic game with you! Thanks to context memory, generative AI tools are particularly adept at word and guessing games, but they can also create fun and challenging trivia quests and interactive stories.

Set Up Your Initial Request

AI is a great partner for playing games when you're on your own. It will play whatever (and whenever) you want, it will abide by your rules, and it never gets bored! AI tools like ChatGPT are most adept with word games or games requiring creativity as a core element. The following are a sampling of seven games you can successfully engage AI with one-on-one, but there are certainly more! Because each of these games can be set up with a single prompt and played from there, there is no necessary starter prompt.

Additional Ways to Personalize

Play One-Word Stories

For fans of wordplay and storytelling, a game of One-Word Stories can be a fun way to pass the time. This classic game consists of you and a partner (or a whole group) telling a story, just one word at a time, with one person saying a word, then the next person adding another word. But what if you have no one to play with? That's where ChatGPT comes in. Want your story to evolve faster? Adapt your prompt to "one-sentence stories." In your prompt you can also provide parameters of the rough type or genre of story you'd like to tell together.

Play a game with me! Together, we will tell a story, but it is only told one word at a time. For example, I'll start with one word like "once," then you'll say the next word, "upon," I'll say "a," you'll say "time," and so on until we've told a whole story. For this story, our theme should be "mystery." Ready?

Play 21 Questions

If you enjoy a good guessing game, you've probably played 21 Questions before—someone thinks of an answer, then the other person asks 21 yes-or-no questions to try to guess what it is. You can either let ChatGPT come up with a secret thing to guess, or you can try to stump ChatGPT. If you want your game to remain broad, keep the instructions as such, but if you're interested in narrowing things to a particular theme, identify that theme in your prompt.

Let's play a game of 21 Questions themed around the world of Harry Potter. You think of a thing, and I will try to guess what it is by asking yes-or-no questions. Count the guesses for me. If I win by getting it right within 21 questions, then you'll have to guess my thing! Let's start!

Play Word Ladder

Word Ladder can be a fun game to test your vocabulary, logic, and problem-solving skills. If you have kids, it's also a fun way to explore and learn new words. The premise of the game is that you have a "starting" and "ending" word, both with the same number of letters. Transforming only one letter at a time, you must transform one word into the other so that you change the first word into the last word. You can choose to play this as a back-and-forth with ChatGPT, or you can ask ChatGPT to give you your starting and ending words and track your progress as you go it alone.

Let's play Word Ladder, where we start with a 5-letter word and end with a totally different 5-letter word by taking turns changing only one letter of the original word at a time. I would like you to begin by picking both starting and ending 5-letter words.

Emoji Interpretation Game

The Emoji Interpretation game is yet another creative guessing game that can be fun for a variety of ages to play. In this game, someone chooses an over-arching subject, like popular movies, TV shows, songs, or books. Then players may describe something from that subject using only emojis for the other player to guess. ChatGPT can generate these emoji-stream prompts for you to guess.

> Let's play a game called Emoji Interpretation. In this game, you'll think of a popular movie and then explain the movie using only emojis (about 5 to 10 max.) Then I must try to guess the movie. I can ask for hints if I need them.

Name That Lyric

Music lover? Challenge your music knowledge with a fun game of Name That Lyric. Ask ChatGPT to give you the first few lines of a popular song, and see how quickly you can guess the song. You can go general with any song or make it specific to genres you particularly love like rock 'n' roll, musical theater, or the nineties. Can't guess it in the first go? Keep asking for the next few lines of music to see if you can guess it. For a similar game, movie buffs can turn this into Name That Movie and be presented with famous lines from films to guess.

> Let's play Name That Lyric. You give me the first 2–4 lines of lyrics from a popular song, and I'll try to guess the song. If I get it right, congratulate me, then give me the next one. No repeats.

General Trivia

Do you love a trivia night out with friends? Sharpen your trivia skills with ChatGPT. For a general trivia game, emphasize in your prompt that the trivia can span all topics and categories. Want to focus on something more specific? Just provide the high-level category the questions should fit within. Keep in mind that more niche themes tend to result in a higher level of hallucination (due to less training in the model).

You are QuizMaster GPT, an AI specialized in generating incredible trivia questions across a variety of difficulty levels and every imaginable general trivia category. You are quizzing me to prepare for the ultimate trivia showdown. Ask me one question at a time, then let me answer. Once I've answered, reveal the correct answer. If my answer was incorrect, explain to me why I was wrong and how I can remember the answer for next time.

Play Choose Your Own Adventure

If you were an avid fan of Choose Your Own Adventure books or video game simulations, you can experience the fun of interactive storytelling with ChatGPT. What makes it even better than books and video games is that you can customize your chosen adventure to whatever environment you want. Detail your instructions, the scenario of the game (get as specific as you'd like!), and the number of options from which you'd like to choose for every narration. Finally, if you are enjoying your game and ChatGPT ends your adventure, you can simply ask it to "continue the game" to keep the journey going.

You are a text-based Choose Your Own Adventure video game where you give me options (A, B, C, and D) as my choices. The scene is in the world of Star Wars but takes place on a new planet not yet experienced in the films. With each choice I make, the scene continues to play out.

CONDUCT A ROLE-PLAY

How AI Can Help You Play Pretend and Engage with Any Character

In our childhoods, most of us let our imaginations run wild, inventing new games to play solo or with friends. By adulthood, though, we tend to abandon the practice of playing pretend, even though many studies have shown play and playfulness in adulthood can have positive impacts on creativity, stress levels, and adaptiveness. And on top of that…it's just plain *fun*! A major obstacle to this playfulness can be finding another adult to participate. And that's where ChatGPT can come in, taking on the role of another character of your choice, in almost any scenario you like!

Set Up Your Initial Request

Your first request will require a little bit of imagination on your part. But if you are at a total loss, you can of course always *ask* ChatGPT to come up with potential scenarios and characters. In your prompt to set up your role-play scenario, inform ChatGPT of its character (and its character's relationship to you) with whatever level of detail you'd like.

Are they your best friend? Your archnemesis? Your romantic interest? Your partner in crime? Is there a particular personality you'd like them to have? If this character is totally of your own creation, you may choose to provide context on their backstory or the situation of their world (or you can ask ChatGPT to create this for you). If you'd like to imagine yourself interacting with a favorite character from a book or film, you can even use that as inspiration!

Sample Starter Prompt

You are Mr. Darcy, the character from Jane Austen's *Pride and Prejudice*. You speak in a formal, eloquent, and refined tone, like that of all aristocrats of Jane Austen's time. Your speech is often short and to the point, like the character in the book. Your character traits include being arrogant and proud, fiercely protective of those you love, and reserved with strangers. I will play the role of Elizabeth Bennet. We have not yet met.

Additional Ways to Personalize

Refine the Character

After you have begun to engage with the character you have developed for ChatGPT to play, you may wish to adjust its responses. Perhaps it is being overly lengthy in its responses and you'd like it to be more conversational. Maybe its responses are too eager and you need it to be more distant. Or maybe some word or phrase choices seem off, or you need to further detail how the tool should feel about your character. In your feedback prompts, clarify that you are putting a pause on the role-play and provide feedback in double parentheses before continuing.

((You are doing great so far. However, I need you to adjust your character: I need your answers short and to the point. As our characters get to know each other, you can begin to open up more. You need not end all your responses in a question—Mr. Darcy would not do that.))

Evolve Your Scenario or Scene

After you have established a starting conversation and shaped your character in the way that is suitable, you can continue to coach the role-play however you'd like. In your prompt, you may choose to provide a detailed scenario, setting, or mission. In subsequent prompts, teach ChatGPT to recognize that certain symbols in your conversation mean different things. For example, [brackets] could indicate a physical action your character (or ChatGPT's) takes, or *asterisks* could indicate each character's inner thoughts. Want to provide more instructions to ChatGPT? Continue to provide them in ((double parentheses)).

((We are at an estate ball filled with loud music, merriment, and dancing. From now on, our characters will share their inner thoughts using asterisks, like so: *inner thoughts*, in addition to still sharing our out-loud dialogue with each other in "quotations". If our characters are taking an action in the scene, this should be expressed in [brackets]. For example: [I look over my shoulder in surprise] "How are you today?" [I smile] *I hate small talk*)).

Illustrate the Scene or Character

Ignite your creativity further by leveraging AI to make images that illustrate the scenes that are playing out within your back-and-forth with ChatGPT. You can either provide a very specific prompt describing the scene, characters, and images you would like to see, or, if you are using an AI with image-generation capabilities for this chat, you can harness its context memory to make an image of the scene as you are playing it out!

((Please make an image of this particular moment in our scene in the style of a regency-era painting.))

GET INSPIRED

How AI Can Help Spark Your Creativity

Because of its excellent brainstorming capabilities, many artists of all types turn to AI to enhance their creativity, inspire new pieces of physical art, or even challenge them creatively. If you ever feel stuck in a creative rut, or you need a little push to get started with your next creative task, you can leverage AI as a helpful collaborator and inspirational coach.

Set Up Your Initial Request

Sometimes you need some ideas to get your creative juices flowing. AI has an unending supply and can tailor them to the type of art you want to pursue.

There is no sample starter prompt for this section because each prompt will vary based on your needs. Start with any of these prompts as an example, then continue to ideate with ChatGPT from there or simply request "more ideas, please!" and it will acquiesce.

Additional Ways to Personalize

Generate Writing Prompts

If you enjoyed creative writing classes as a student but have not written in a long time, or if you enjoy writing as a hobby but are stuck with writer's block, ChatGPT can provide you with multiple varied starting points for your next creative tasks. In your prompt, you can ask for one idea or multiple ideas. For a wider variety of ideas, you can avoid specificity. To receive ideas that fit within a more refined subcategory, define the higher-level parameters in your prompt, like "Just ideas for poetry," or "Creative writing for mundane scenarios," or "sci-fi genre."

> Give me 10 specific, descriptive, unique, and varied writing prompts. All should be fantastical fictional scenarios or scenes.

Refine Writing Prompts with a Specific Challenge

By narrowing down your choices so you don't have unlimited options, you can sharpen your focus and push past analysis paralysis in your creative process. With AI, you can request specific challenges or bounds for your creative writing or other artistic creations. ChatGPT can challenge you with different structural recommendations for a poem or generate random things you must incorporate into your next task.

> Now give me up to 10 very specific and varied challenges when writing the scenarios above. Examples include: Give me 3 random words I must incorporate into the story, give me 2 unrelated objects to include, give me a description of a character to introduce, and so on.

Suggest Objects to Draw or Sculpt

Are you a skilled artist or simply a hobbyist with a knack for painting, drawing, or sculpting? You can similarly leverage ChatGPT to suggest ideas and challenges for your next work of art. Detail what type of art you are trying to create and ask it to recommend a scene, challenge, or detail to incorporate into your next work.

> I am developing my painting skills, and I work primarily in acrylics. Please give me 5 detailed, descriptive, and unique painting challenges to consider for my next painting. These should all broadly be "landscapes."

Get Visual Inspiration for Your Challenge As Well

If a descriptive written challenge is not quite enough to inspire your next work, or if you'd prefer visual inspiration, you can take your artistic challenge one step further by having AI generate an image based on the very prompt it has just given you! Simply copy and paste the suggestion into any AI image-generating tool (if you are already conversing with the tool, skip this step). Then ask it to "make an image" of the prompt in the artistic style you hope to create.

> Make a horizontal image of an acrylic painting of <paste in AI's previous prompt here>.

Generate AI Image As Craft Inspiration

Maybe you already have a loose idea of what you'd like to create but want some help generating concepts for an "end result." AI is not limited to 2-D drawing and painting inspiration! From cross-stitch and needlepoint designs to pottery and quilts, you can use AI image generation to inspire these types of arts and crafts as well.

> Generate a picture of a patchwork quilt with geometric patterns inspired by the night sky.
>
> Create an image of a very interesting ceramic pot that has realistic but unique nature-inspired attributes for me to use as inspiration for a pot to create. Temperature 0.9.

LEARN ABOUT RANDOM STORIES FROM HISTORY

If you love to learn about little-known but interesting stories and tidbits from history, AI can be a great partner in expanding your knowledge of random facts. This can also be a handy way to entertain people (or just yourself!) during long stretches of boredom, like on road trips! Just turn on ChatGPT's voice feature for your prompts and to hear ChatGPT's responses read aloud. You can ask for a totally random subject matter or refine your prompt to ask for specific times in history or categories like inventors, women in history, cultural practices, or anything else!

> I need you to generate random but little-known real stories from history. I am specifically looking for stories that were not likely taught in-depth in a traditional high school curriculum in America. Start with a random story, giving me lots of interesting details. When I am ready for a new random (and unrelated) story, I will tell you.

SUGGEST STYLING TIPS FOR OUTFITS

Have you ever bought a new clothing item after absolutely falling in love with it at the store, but then you realize…you have no idea what to wear it with or how you might style it? Snap a photo of you wearing the item in question and upload it into an AI tool with vision capabilities to ask for styling suggestions.

> I recently bought this oversized long-sleeved collared shirt (as shown in the picture). I typically just wear it tucked into jeans, but the outfit is nothing to write home about. Could you give me 10 specific ideas of new ways to style or accessorize this shirt to create new looks and styles throughout multiple seasons?

WRITE SILLY POEMS OR SONG LYRICS

AI can be a great entertainer, crafting song lyrics or poetry about any topic or situation you can imagine. Simply detail in your prompt the topic or subject matter of the song or poem, the musical or poetic style the lyrics or structure should reflect, and any other important details. Want to write a whole song, with music *and* lyrics? There are AI tools, like Suno AI, that can do exactly that!

Write song lyrics inspired by doo-wop-style rock 'n' roll music about getting off work on a Friday after a long week and discovering that there is no beer left in your fridge.

TRANSFORM YOUR PICTURES INTO CARTOONS

Want a fun party trick? Snap a photo of your friends or pets and upload it into a generative AI tool with a prompt on how to create a new image inspired by the original, in whatever artistic style you request. You do not necessarily need to snap the photo yourself, and you can rely entirely on your written prompt, but by uploading your own image, you can save time on the exact details of your prompt. The AI tool will use your uploaded image as guidance on its output, taking cues from your uploaded image's lighting and style to guide the image it creates.

Reimagine the dog in this picture as a Pixar-animated movie poster. The dog in your image should look just like this dog and be in the same pose. However, in your image, the dog should be on the beach and wearing sunglasses.

GET PERSONALIZED ENTERTAINMENT SUGGESTIONS

Have you ever caught yourself spending more time aimlessly scrolling through options on a streaming service than it would have taken you to watch a single episode of a TV show? There are so many options for entertainment these days across movies, TV, books, and more that choosing something can feel overwhelming, especially since there is no guarantee you'll end up liking what you choose! ChatGPT can help you narrow your decision by providing a personalized list of recommendations based on your preferences or needs. Just give some examples of content that you do like and why, and ask ChatGPT to provide further suggestions while explaining why it may be a good option for you.

I'm looking for 10 personalized suggestions for new TV shows to watch. While I don't necessarily need a pure comedy, I do want a show that has opportunities for laughter sprinkled throughout. Some of my favorite shows include *Breaking Bad* (for the characterization and incredible storytelling), *Parks and Recreation* (so funny! Great characters, and uplifting energy), *The Good Place* (funny but also invites me to think about things in a new way), and *Westworld* (great world-building, interesting plot). For each recommendation, detail (1) a summary of what the show is about, (2) why you think I might like it, and (3) roughly how long an episode is.

Index

Note: Page numbers in parentheses indicate intermittent references.